START SOMETHING TO END TRAFFICKING

A PRACTICAL GUIDE TO HELP YOU START
A PROJECT, EVENT, CAMPAIGN, OR ORGANIZATION

by David Trotter

Awaken Media

START SOMETHING TO END TRAFFICKING: A Practical Guide to Help You Start a Project, Event, Campaign, or Organization
by David Trotter

© 2014 by Awaken Media. All rights reserved. No part of this publication may be reproduced or transmitted in any form or by any means without written permission of the publisher.

Designed by 8TRACKstudios - www.8trackstudios.com

ISBN: 978-1-935798-11-8

To the ones who love me,
support me, and listen to my long-winded
updates around the dinner table about
all the "somethings" I start.

Thank you Laura, Waverly, and Emerson
for your love and support.

TABLE OF CONTENTS

Introduction - Don't Get Stuck in Traffick — 7

Chapter 1 - Why Do You Want to Start Something? — 17
  Find your "why" before anything else.

Chapter 2 - What Are You Trying to Accomplish? — 27
  Get clear about your "something".

Chapter 3 - How to Launch a PROJECT — 39
  Ask yourself (and others) the right questions.

Chapter 4 - How to Host an EVENT — 53
  Create an experience everyone will be talking about.

Chapter 5 - How to Raise Money Through a CAMPAIGN — 67
  Be clear about your "ask" and invite people to give.

Chapter 6 - How to Start an ORGANIZATION — 81
  Get serious about longer-term impact.

Chapter 7 - Recruit and Motivate Your Team — 91
  Rally a team to help make it happen.

Chapter 8 - Market Your Something — 101
  Use every possible means to spread the word.

Chapter 9 - Refine, Replicate, Rejuvenate — 119
  Learn from the experience and take care of your soul.

DON'T GET STUCK IN TRAFFICK

I live in southern California where traffic is a way of life. Thousands upon thousands of people everywhere...and almost every single one of them has a car...or two. No matter where I go, I'm surrounded by *traffic*.

People from out of town ask, "How long does it take to get to the airport?"

"Well, it depends on what time you go. It could take 30 minutes or it could take an hour and a half."

If you're driving between 6:45-9am, expect *traffic*.
Between 11:45am-1pm, expect *traffic*.
After 3:30 and before 7pm, expect *traffic*.

Traffic is assumed; yet, it's something all of us do our best to avoid. We hate the inconvenience and the headache of daily congestion, and the last thing we want to be is...*stuck* in traffic.

Stuck behind an accident.
Stuck in bumper-to-bumper gridlock.
Stuck in the unending construction of the 5 Freeway.

We do whatever we can to steer clear of it, but there's no denying that it exists. It's everywhere.

Human traffick-ing is no different.

START SOMETHING TO END TRAFFICKING

It's uncomfortable, inconvenient, and gut wrenching, and most of us simply want to avoid it.

Trafficking in all its forms - labor, sex, and organ - is extremely disturbing to the average person. When our friends and family hear about it on the news, they're quick to either turn the channel to avoid the pain or gawk in disbelief as if they're staring at mangled cars involved in a roadside wreck.

"How could someone sell another human being?"
"At what point did these creeps think this was okay?"
"I just can't deal with this!"

Many of us mentally drive around the subject to avoid dealing with the reality that it's happening in our world...in our country...and even in our own city. We come up with some kind of intellectual excuse that makes us feel better about circumnavigating the issue.

"She's just a prostitute who wants to sell herself."
"Why don't these people try to escape? They could just walk away."
"There's absolutely no way this is happening in our area!"

Feel better now that you've avoided it? Some people actually do, and they lull themselves to sleep at the wheel thinking this isn't an issue that impacts their daily lives...kinda like someone in my area trying to convince themselves that road traffic isn't really that bad. You might be able to live in that world for a short time, but eventually you'll start to experience the reality of the issue.

At the same time, those of us who *have* recognized the trafficking epidemic can feel so overwhelmed that we feel stuck. I say "we", because my guess is that you and I would be more prone to fit into this category. You wouldn't be reading this book unless you realized that human trafficking is an issue our world needs to deal with...*now*.

It can be overwhelming, can't it?

I'll admit it. I can feel defeated by the issue of human trafficking. If it's *really* happening here, there, and practically everywhere...where do I even begin? My mind spins out with the complexity of the issue, my heart is heavy with sadness for the victim, anger toward the perpetrators, and embarrassment for my own naive participation in the process.

INTRODUCTION

With all of that swirling in and around me,
I can start to feel stuck...*stuck in traffick*.

Whether people feel *stuck* in their questioning if human trafficking really is a big deal or *stuck* with overwhelming emotions as they deal with the complexity of the issue, they usually respond in one of three ways to the issue.

1. A few people stay stuck in traffick.
Most of us hate feeling *stuck* about anything, so we avoid the experience at all costs. If we feel overwhelmed, inconvenienced, and unable to move, we usually move toward option 2 or 3 to "unstick" ourselves.

2. Many people avoid human traffick-ing.
To avoid dealing with the issue, many choose to believe it's not that bad. They think it's someone else's responsibility, and they turn their attention to something that's more pleasant...like what's on Netflix.

3. More and more people are helping to end human traffick-ing.
For many of us, once we became aware of the issue of human trafficking, there's no way we could retreat into our cozy homes and forget about those whose lives are ravaged by people who are singularly focused on profit and pleasure at the expense of other human beings. We *have* to do something about it. We *have* to end traffick-ing. This is the response to traffick that we want to invite more and more people to have. We want them to join us in helping to end traffick-ing altogether.

In December of 1994, I boarded a plane to India with 30 or so adventurous souls including Stephanie Pollaro and Wendy Dailey - just hours after the tsunami struck the eastern coast of our destination. We were headed on a humanitarian trip to visit remote villages in what ended up being several hours from the devastation.

During our two-week trip, we had the opportunity to visit a red light district in Tenali, Andhra Pradesh, where two men own over 50 women. To the outsider, it looks like nothing more than a long row of concrete floor, thatch roof huts along a deep ditch filled with stagnant, trash-strewn water. To locals, it's known as the place you go to purchase sex. As we walked down the dirt road, our translators pointed out the long colorful fabric hung from rope - stretched from tree to tree - blocking the view from the main road so that customers are given some sense of privacy as they arrive.

START SOMETHING TO END TRAFFICKING

While I stood next to one of the owners (pimps/traffickers), Stephanie had the opportunity to stand in front of all the women (victims) who were gathered together to receive saris - a small gift from our team. As she shared God's love for each of the women, her eyes welled up with tears that soon flooded down her face. While all of us were touched by the plight of these women, something even more powerful happened within Stephanie and Wendy. It was on that trip that a seed was planted in their hearts that ultimately germinated into what has become iSanctuary, founded in 2007 to provide holistic care for women and girls through job training, education, and medical care.

Currently, they have a program in Mumbai, India, for women and girls aged 12-25, rescued from sexual slavery. Through the program, girls are able to create a better life for themselves and obtain true freedom by making a line of fashion jewelry (called Purpose - www.purposejewelry.org) that earns them double the fair trade in India. The other half of their program is based in Orange County, California, where U.S. survivors of sex trafficking participate in a nine month program providing job readiness, computer skills training, and professional development - all happening as the women prepare, package, and ship the jewelry made by survivors in India.

100% of the proceeds from Purpose jewelry benefit the survivors through iSanctuary. Purchases provide employment, job training, and the financial stability survivors need in order to properly provide for themselves and their families. Each young woman who graduates from the program at iSanctuary is equipped with the skills and knowledge that she needs to enter the job market with confidence.

Although the process to launch iSanctuary literally took years, Stephanie and Wendy just *had* to do something to stop traffick-ing.

It's doubtful that traffic in southern California will ever end, but human traffick-ing *must* end for the sake of humankind. If we allow ourselves and those in our communities to stay stuck or avoid the issue of human trafficking in our world, we will continue to participate (directly or indirectly) in the trafficking of precious lives.

I Had to Start Something
When I first heard about human trafficking, I have to admit that I avoided the traffick. I thought of it as a distant problem, until I witnessed it first

INTRODUCTION

hand in Thailand and India as women and children were being blatantly sold for sex with no effort to cover up the heinous business. Then, on a business trip to China, I was invited by my hosts to an underground karaoke suite after dinner, and 20 or so girls were escorted onto the stage - all dressed in traditional Chinese outfits and looking quite beautiful.

While I'm not sure of their ages, most appeared to be older teens or 20-somethings, and they were smiling at us as if nothing was wrong. Within a matter of moments, I was asked which one I wanted to spend the evening with. After declining, my hosts said, "Ah. I see...you must want a boy!" as the room filled with laughter.

Really? This is the type of world we live in?

Soon thereafter, I started to hear about the issue of sex trafficking in the United States. My mind was stretched to capacity when I heard that children and women were being sold for sex in my own area, and I knew that I *had* to do something.

After a positive experience with the distributor of my first documentary, I re-approached Word Entertainment about the possibility of a project focused on domestic sex trafficking, and they were incredibly receptive. Through a relationship with Hope for Justice (www.hopeforjustice.org) and Natalie Grant (www.nataliegrant.com), I had the opportunity to assemble a team and produce a compelling, hope-filled film on six female abolitionists who are fighting to end sex trafficking in the United States. In the process of making *IN PLAIN SIGHT: Stories of Hope and Freedom*, I became impassioned to educate people on the issue of trafficking and motivate them to take action in their own communities.

As people watch the film and are educated on the issue, I keep hearing, *"I want to do something, but I'm not sure what to do or how to do it."*

I'm especially hearing this from college students, 20-somethings, and beyond - people with a great deal of passion, skill, and time who want to invest themselves in something that truly matters. If you have this book in your hands, I'm talking about you! You've become aware of human trafficking, and you want to do something about it. You don't want to remain stuck or avoid the traffick. Wearing a t-shirt and posting on Instagram are fine for some, but you want to go to the next level.

START SOMETHING TO END TRAFFICKING

You want to *start* something to *end* trafficking.

I know the feeling. I've been a starter my entire life. I love starting things, and I love doing things in a unique way. That's not to say that I don't like working with existing organizations, because I do. I've started quite a few businesses and non-profits over the course of my 40+ years of life, and it's a pain in the butt and a lot of work. Oftentimes, it's easier and more effective to come alongside an existing organization to help them accomplish their mission rather than starting another organization from scratch.

That's what I did with the IN PLAIN SIGHT documentary. It would have been virtually impossible for me to produce that film without the help of Hope for Justice, an existing non-profit with a network of aftercare homes throughout the United States.

If our crew of three guys would have cold-called a list of sex trafficking aftercare homes to pitch the idea of shooting a documentary on their properties, my guess is we wouldn't have gotten very far. On the other hand, by partnering with an existing organization, we were able to come alongside each home in a way that complimented their mission and allowed us to create something that benefits the entire anti-trafficking movement.

All that to say, there are hundreds of wonderful organizations that have already been started to help end human trafficking in our world. Perhaps you are feeling called to start one yourself. May I suggest that you consider leveraging your energy (and entrepreneurial skills) by working within an *existing* organization. Imagine an event, project, or campaign that would benefit what someone else is already doing.

If we start to partner with one another even more than we are now, we can create powerful organizations (non-profits, churches, businesses, schools, etc.) that are truly addressing this issue - rather than launching a bunch of random groups focused on raising awareness. Don't get me wrong - raising awareness is a good thing. In large part, that's what IN PLAIN SIGHT is all about, but I recognized that I don't need to start another organization to do that. I had the privilege of partnering with existing, credible organizations, and that might be something you consider as well.

Why I Wrote This Book For You
Over the past 20+ years, I've started churches, businesses, and non-profits, and within each of those, I've started events, projects, and campaigns. As

INTRODUCTION

an entrepreneurial soul, many of the things I've started have not gone as I'd wished, but many have made an impact in ways far beyond my wildest dreams. One of the things that people ask me time and again is, "How the heck are you able to pull that off? How do you get so much done in such little time?" Frankly, I must have them fooled, because I always find myself saying, "Good grief, this took waaaaay longer and it was waaaaay harder than I ever dreamed!"

I start something thinking - "oh this is no big deal" - and end up realizing that it's more intense than I could have imagined. Thankfully, I don't always see all the hard work in front of me, because I'm not sure I would actually set out to do extraordinary things if I did.

Seven years ago, I transitioned out of being a full-time pastor (having led and started churches for 10 years), and I have leveraged my skills to help others in a variety of ways. To give you an idea of my experience with "starting" things, here's just a glimpse of how I've served in the last seven years...

- Co-founded a plush toy manufacturing business that focuses on cause marketing (still in business).
- Launched a marketing boutique that grossed over six figures in the first year (what I do to pay my bills).
- Contracted with developers to create four iPhone apps (still in the app store except for one that may have slightly infringed on a copyright by a major gaming company...whoops!).
- Wrote and published a memoir, a self-help book with accompanying workbook, two photography books, and a Christian inspiration book (all available on Amazon).
- Hired by three separate clients to ghost-write their books.
- Travelled to India four times - including once with my family of four to visit the children's home we helped start with some friends.
- Produced my first documentary *(Mother India: Life Through the Eyes of the Orphan)* with global distribution through Word Films.
- Spoke at multiple US churches and for a crowd of 20,000 in India.
- Produced my second documentary featuring six female abolitionists *(In Plain Sight: Stories of Hope and Freedom)* with global distribution through Word Films.
- Co-executive produced an accompany benefit album and co-wrote a 31 day devotional and group study guide.

- And, celebrated 20 years of marriage with an amazing wife as we raise our two children in partnership.

Although I've had a lot of fun starting many things, the last point on that list is the one I'm most proud of. My wife is my partner (practically a saint) for letting me pursue my dreams and passions, and my family keeps me grounded in ways that are healing and refreshing for my soul. I love them dearly.

After reading that list, you may be wondering...*Who does this guy think he is starting all this stuff? Who gave this guy permission to start a business? Who said it was okay to dream about an iPhone app and find inexpensive ways to pull it off? Who said it was okay for him to write and publish books?*

No one. Over time, something started to germinate within me that *wanted* to do these things, so I just figured out how to do it...and I invested my time and energy to make it happen.

Had you ever ghost-written a book before? Did you know how to produce a documentary? Was there any guarantee it would be distributed globally?

No, no, and no.

Who are you to produce a documentary on sex trafficking in the US? Aren't there people way more qualified - both in terms of the subject and in terms of filmmaking? Why would you ever think it was okay to produce a benefit album with major Christian artists donating their songs? Who said you could write a devotional and study guide to go along with the film and album?

You've got to know that I'm not a naturally confident person who thinks I can do whatever I set out to do. Unfortunately, my self-talk sounds more like, "Who do you think you are? There are thousands of other people more gifted to do _____. Nobody knows who you are, and they're not going to be interested in what you have to offer. Don't even think about it!"

Ugh. I hate those voices. Those are all "lies" that seek to steal, kill, and destroy the Divine dreams and passions that have been planted inside of me...and you.

In my past life as a pastor, I overcompensated for these lies by becoming a workaholic and putting in 60-70 hours a week for 10 years straight. After a

INTRODUCTION

burnout and a reorienting of my life, I'm still able to use my talents, skills, and experiences - but to serve others *and* love my family. Although there are bursts of intense work during deadlines, I no longer put in those long hours, and I'm extremely available to my family now. Although it can still be a struggle, I've spent the last 20 years learning to tune the antennae of my soul to the "truths" of who God made me to be. Spirituality may or may not be part of your life, but I'm not sure what I would do without mine. My faith orients my mind and heart around the Divine truths that remind me who I *really* am.

Here's an example of how it works for me...

Lie: I am nobody, and I don't have much to offer.
Truth: I am beautifully and wonderfully made by God.

Lie: God is too busy to even think about me.
Truth: God loves me more than I could ever know.

Lie: I am too _____ (young, old, poor, inexperienced, etc.)
Truth: God has given me unique gifts, talents, and experiences.

Lie: It doesn't matter if I get involved or help others.
Truth: God has prepared good works in advance for me to do.

Lie: I don't know where to start, and it's too overwhelming.
Truth: God's Spirit lives within me to guide and encourage me.

Lie: My family doesn't understand me or my dreams.
Truth: My family and friends love me the best they know how.

Lie: I'm just gonna screw this up...why even try?
Truth: I am a life-long learner who isn't expected to be perfect.

Lie: I don't have enough _____ (time, money, volunteers, etc.)
Truth: I have access to all the resources I need.

I have a sneaking suspicion I'm not the only one who hears (and believes) these lies on a daily basis. The only way I could possibly start and successfully complete any of the events, projects, or campaigns listed on the previous pages is by regularly choosing to believe the truths instead of the lies. Many people never even get to the point of dreaming, because the lies have robbed them of the ability to think they can do something beyond the ordinary.

That's not you though. You haven't stopped dreaming. In fact, you picked up this book, because you believe you can do something to help end human trafficking in our world. Consider me an ally in that fight. I believe in you and the fact that God has given you a unique set of talents, skills, and experiences you can leverage for the benefit of those who are being ravaged for the profit and pleasure of others.

Now, let's get down to the business at hand.

You have a desire to start "something." You want to help, but you're not quite sure how. That's what this book is all about.

I want to share with you how I do what I do. For some of you, what I'm about to share will seem simple, because you've been starting things your entire life. Search for the nuggets of inspiration, and may your heart and mind be refueled. For others, this book may feel incredibly stretching, because this is all new for you. Hang in there, and lean in to the learning process.

What I'm about to share with you isn't the *only* way or *best* way or *guaranteed* way, but it happens to be the methodology I've developed over the last 20 years that works for *me*. While I will be "prescriptive" as I share my approach with you, you'll need to find your own way. You'll need to find what works for you, and the only way to figure that out is by actually doing it!

By the end of this book, I want you to feel equipped to start an event, project, or campaign specifically focused on something to help end human trafficking in our world. Heck…you may even start an organization!

Are you ready? Let's dive in.

Chapter One

WHY DO YOU WANT TO START SOMETHING?

During her junior year of high school, Anna Merzi was eagerly searching for a cause that would empower her to make a difference in the world. After attending a seminar on human trafficking, she left the meeting in absolute shock at the prevalence of human trafficking on a global scale and within her own Texas community.

"I had this idea that if only more people knew about these atrocities, it could be stopped in just one generation. There was something about the human trafficking cause that felt empowering. It was right in my backyard, but it was a global problem. It didn't matter how small I felt, I couldn't sit idle. Being afraid of the traffickers' power only gave them more strength. You can't fight human trafficking quietly, you have to get up and prove to the world that it can be stopped. Then, the fight is contagious, and then we become bigger than the crime itself."

Using her school's chapter of Junior State of America (a high school civics and leadership program) as a platform, Anna set out to use mainstream media to raise awareness among her peers. First, she created a trafficking fast-facts Twitter page for her high school and gave out prizes for individuals who discussed the tweets at the school's weekly JSA meetings. Then, she hosted a screening in her high school's auditorium of an episode of Law and Order SVU about child prostitution and gave away free Chick-fil-A sandwiches to attendees. During prom season, she spoke at an all-school assembly regarding human trafficking at nail salons, and she gave out a list of red flags to look our for, as well as a list of salons that were confirmed to use fair employment standards.

Once Anna became aware of the problem, she could not remain idle. She had to do something. Why? Because she knew she could make a difference right where she lived. She was needed, and her efforts made a difference.

The Power of Asking "Why"
When we ask the question "why", we're invited to reflect on the very reason we do anything in life - why we think a certain way, why we feel a particular emotion, or why we choose to take action...or not.

The question "why" presupposes there is a deeper meaning or motivation behind whatever is being considered. The reality is that we do *everything* in life for a reason. Sometimes, those reasons are rather flimsy ("I just like to do it") while other times the reasons are quite dense ("this is the way my family has always done it").

Think with me for a moment about the reason why you do some of the most common things in life.

- Why do you start your day with _____?
- Why do you drive a particular type of car?
- Why do you work at your current job?
- Why do you spend the holidays with _____?

There is an underlying reason "why" for every one of these questions. If we live an unexamined life, we'll make decisions about almost everything without much regard for the motivating factors.

Let's take something as simple as the car you drive. I have several friends who are struggling financially with the current economy, but when it comes time to acquire a care, they always purchase a luxury brand. With only a couple hundred dollars a month for a payment, they opt for the Mercedes or BMW or Range Rover with 100,000 miles on it versus a Toyota or Ford or Chevy that's much newer.

Why do they make that choice?

Why Do You Want to Start Something?

I'm not in their shoes, but from the outside, it seems like they are wanting to project an image they aspire to, but aren't able to fully live up to in the midst of their financial challenges. It's not really any of my business why they make that choice, but it motivates me to ask "why" in my own life.

Why do I choose to lease two brand new cars versus any number of other options?

On the surface, I could say that I just like the cars. Yet, if I ask the deeper "why" of myself, I can be honest and say that I want to avoid the stress I saw my parents experience when our used cars would break down. I want power locks and leather seats and USB plugs and nice floor mats, because my parents avoided that stuff as impractical or something that might break. I don't want to worry about maintenance costs...and everyone in Orange County seems to have a new car, so I should probably have one, too.

Whew! That was pretty honest, huh? Once I reflect on my "why", I'm left to ask myself, "Do I still want to make that same decision next time? Do I feel comfortable with my motivations? Do they align or resonate with my overall values in life?"

That's just from asking "why" I drive a particular car. Think about how helpful that can be with other aspects of life - including why you want to start something to help end human trafficking in our world.

Your "Why" Started at Home

You can learn all the strategies and tactics about starting something, but it will only take you so far without first understanding your underlying belief systems that motivate your actions. The beliefs we have about ourselves, others, and our world ultimately construct our reality. What we believe is largely influenced by our home of origin - the environment in which we were raised. This may have been with both parents or a single mom or grandparents or foster homes or any number of other situations.

Our homes of origin provide us with our initial beliefs about...

- The presence of love and hate in our world.
- What is right or wrong in terms of thoughts, attitudes, and behavior.
- Our role in responding to social justice issues.
- Whether we see ourselves as a leader or entrepreneur.
- How faith is part or not part of our worldview.

- And, ultimately, the purpose or meaning of life.

If your parents taught you (subtly or explicitly) that you can't trust people because they're out to get you, that's going to impact how you live life.

If your home of origin communicated that it's someone else's responsibility to handle "that problem", you'll have a particular outlook on the challenges of our world.

If you were raised in an environment where going to school, getting a steady job, and living for the weekend was modeled and celebrated, your perspective on vocation, work, and entrepreneurialvolunteerism will have been shaped.

I'm hesitant to label most of these beliefs as right, wrong, good, or bad, but I *am* interested in seeing if they might be "unhelpful" in some way. Are you getting the results you truly want by maintaining your current "whys" about life?

Here's the reason why the beliefs you hold about yourself, others, and the world at large are so important.

> **BELIEFS determine your**
> **ACTIONS which produce your**
> **RESULTS which impact your**
> **EMOTIONAL STATE.**

Because our emotions are involved throughout the entire cycle of beliefs, actions, and results, this isn't a purely linear process, but let's break this down.

- **BELIEFS determine your ACTIONS.**
  Every action that you and I take is based on a belief...it's rooted in a "why." You believe a chair will hold you, so you take the action of sitting down. You believe it's ethical to hand back the extra dollar the cashier accidentally gave you, so you choose to bring it to his or her attention. You believe that people are inherently valuable and should not be forced to do something against their will, so you choose to take action on behalf of those who are being trafficked. Your belief is your "why", and it determines how you take action...or whether you take action at all (which, in reality, is an action in and of itself).

Why Do You Want to Start Something?

- **ACTIONS produce your RESULTS.**
  When you take action, there will be a result. It may not be the exact result you wanted, but it will bring about a change in your life. By believing that the chair will hold you, you choose to sit down, and the result is physical relief on your feet, legs, and back. By believing that it's ethical to give back extra money, you choose to bring it to his or her attention, and the result is an expression of appreciation on the part of the cashier who could have been reprimanded for the financial loss. By believing that people have inherent value, you choose to take action on behalf of those who are trafficked, and the result is a victim's life is saved or transformed. See how that works?

- **RESULTS impact your EMOTIONAL STATE.**
  Although your beliefs about yourself, others, and the world at large will impact how you feel, nothing impacts our emotional state more than tangible results. By sitting down (rooted in your belief that the chair will hold you), you experience physical and emotional relief. By handing the extra dollar back to the cashier, you will experience deep satisfaction, because your actions lined up with your beliefs. By taking action on behalf of those who are trafficked, you have the opportunity to feel fulfilled in doing something on behalf of another.

When you experience a positive emotional state, your beliefs and actions are affirmed, and you want to continue repeating the process. Ironically, if you have a negative result and negative emotional response, it will cause you to question your belief - the "why" behind your actions.

We go through most of our days unaware of the underlying beliefs we have about life, but they are there nonetheless. In moments like these (when we're seeking to take intentional action), it is always best to start with "why". Otherwise, we may find ourselves down the road - aimlessly starting an event, project, campaign, or organization for a reason that isn't very helpful to ourselves, survivors, or the anti-trafficking movement at large.

Find Your "Why" Before Anything Else
Now that we understand the power of our "why", let's start to examine some reasons why you and I might want to help end human trafficking in our world.

You may be thinking, "Well, isn't it obvious?!?! People are being tortured and taken advantage of?"

START SOMETHING TO END TRAFFICKING

Yes, you're right. They are, and that's why we're all working to end trafficking, but that's not the *only* reason (or even the primary one) why some of us want to start something. One of my beliefs is that we, as human beings, do things for a variety of reasons - not just one. Rarely, if ever, are those reasons 100% pure and selfless and for the sake of others - and that's okay.

With that in mind, let's be honest about some of the reasons why we may want to start something. Some of these things may not resonate with you, but I'll go ahead and lead the way and admit that these have been motivating factors for me from time to time...

- **I've wanted people to see me as a _____ person.**
  Fill in that blank - good, generous, powerful, creative, smart, or competent. There's nothing wrong with wanting others to see us in a positive light, but when that becomes a primary motivation, it can drive us to live for the opinions of others.

- **I've wanted my Mom and Dad to be proud of me.**
  Who doesn't? A belief that we're "not enough" in some way can often stem from perceptions developed during our growing up years, and we can spend a lifetime trying to make up for it.

- **I've been motivated by pain, anger, and resentment.**
  When we have a hurtful experience at the hands of another person or organization, this can fuel us to act in ways that appear just or righteous or altruistic on the surface. Yet, an undercurrent of negative energy can be fueling us, and eventually it will spew out into whatever we're working on.

- **I've been motivated by jealousy.**
  When we see someone else experiencing success or accolades, we may be tempted to start something to get a dose of that positive energy for ourselves. The truth is that there will always be *someone* ahead of us in one way or another.

- **I've been motivated by guilt.**
  When we feel bad about something - either something we've individually done or something our gender/ethnicity/country has done in the past - we can be driven by a need to relieve those feelings and make up for it in some way. The question is, will starting something make those feelings go away?

Why Do You Want to Start Something?

- **I've been motivated by money.**
  This is a tricky one for sure. Unless we're independently wealthy or have a trust fund we're living off of, most of us need to generate income somehow. Yet, if "getting a paycheck" is our primary motivation for starting something, I'm not sure whatever we start will last if and when money becomes a challenge.

- **I've been motivated to be "somebody".**
  "If I can just do this, then I'll finally be known by others." This thirst for recognition is incredibly tempting in our celebrity culture. Isn't it ironic that our work to help others could be motivated by a desire for personal fame or notoriety?

Once again, I'm hesitant to make a judgment on any of these motivations, but I'm just wondering if they're helpful to us. Are some of these motivations mixed in with my desire to do good in the world? Of course! Yet, I seek to gain an awareness of the reason "why" I'm doing what I'm doing and intentional choose a more helpful motivation if it would be beneficial.

Let's talk about some other "whys" that may be *more* helpful as we seek to start something to help end human trafficking in our world...

- **Human beings are inherently valuable and have equal worth.**
  In my faith, we believe that every human being is created in the image of God, and therefore, they have incredible worth - no matter what their gender, ethnicity, language, education level, or socio-economic situation.

- **No person should ever be bought or sold.**
  People are not objects to be traded or sold for the profit and pleasure of other human beings. Because we have been created in the image of God, there is something uniquely different about human life - versus physical objects or even animals.

- **Coercion, manipulation, abuse, and violence are intolerable.**
  Exploiting another human being because of their vulnerability will tear apart the fabric of our society. It creates an atmosphere of distrust and instability.

- **All three parties involved are in need of restoration.**
  The victim, the trafficker (pimp/seller), and the buyer are all in need

of transformation for different reasons. Being sold, selling, and buying are a result of human brokenness, and these actions result in even more injury to all three parties.

- **Human trafficking can be prevented.**
  By decreasing or eliminating someone's vulnerability, they become unavailable to a trafficker. By instilling a belief in the inherent value of other human beings and creating/enforcing laws that present this truth, people are more prone to stop selling and buying.

- **Each one of us has a role to play to prevent and end trafficking.**
  No matter where we live/work or how old we are or how much money we have or what education level we've attained, we can all do something to stop this heinous crime against humanity, but we do need each other. There's no one person, organization, or government that can eradicate this issue. Everyone is needed, and we must lock arms to tackle it together.

I wonder if *these beliefs* might be more powerful "whys" to start something to end trafficking than the previous list. I think so. How about you?

Motivated by Love
In 1999, Lucy Strausbaugh adopted a 15 year old girl, Nadia, from an institution with a poor reputation in Romania, just months before she would have been evicted from this "orphanage" - unprepared for life and having to try to figure out how to make it on her own. Having learned about Eastern European human trafficking in the early 90's, it dawned on Lucy how vulnerable her new daughter would have been, and this knowledge continues to drive what some call "her persistence in eradicating this scourge."

For the past 38 years, Lucy has taught senior-level Religious Studies classes at Notre Dame Preparatory School in Towson, Maryland, and she now includes education on human trafficking with an emphasis on sex trafficking in particular. Not only does she educate her students on the global issue, but she teaches them how to avoid dangerous situations they may encounter themselves. They are also taught to be on the lookout for younger girls who might be targeted by traffickers and how to call for assistance.

"I've lost count of the emails I've received from current and former students who are traveling, at truck stops, on planes, in airports, and at hotels, who have reported what looks suspiciously like trafficking. They've told me

Why Do You Want to Start Something?

stories of seeing a man dragging a teen girl across the street against her will and a little girl who seemed to be afraid of the man she was traveling with. They have learned that it is better to report something and have it turn out to be nothing, than to live with the thought that they could have been the cause of someone's liberation, but they didn't make the call."

Undoubtedly, Lucy's "why" stems from a love for her daughter and the hundreds of girls she has taught over the past 38 years as a high school teacher.

What's My Motivation?
If my "why" is centered around the opinions of others, what happens when someone is dissatisfied with me and my efforts?

If it's about pleasing my Mom and Dad, what if they don't understand?

If I'm motivated by pain, anger, and resentment, what do I do when things don't go as planned? Get more angry?

If jealousy or guilt are my "whys", will my heart ever be satisfied?

If I'm primarily motivated by money, what happens when funds run short?

And, if I'm looking to gain notoriety, what if no one ever notices my hard work?

In the midst of the events, projects, campaigns, and organizations I've started over the last 20 years, I've been partially motivated by the first list of "whys" from time to time. They are shallow and weak, and they ultimately run out of steam. Yet, as I do my small part to help end human trafficking in our world, I've found the second list of "whys" to be deeper, richer, and more powerful. When I notice I'm getting sidetracked by any of the less helpful motivations, I take a moment to re-orient my heart and intentionally re-affirm my foundational beliefs.

By exploring your "why" and choosing a different motivation if necessary, you're setting yourself up for a better result. Remember, your beliefs determine your actions which produce your results which impact your emotional state.

Let's choose a solid "why" so that our efforts are powerful and the results are long-lasting.

Chapter Two

WHAT ARE YOU TRYING TO ACCOMPLISH?

After asking "why", the next question to ask is "what?" What are you trying to accomplish by starting something? Yes, we all want to end human trafficking, but what *specifically* are you wanting to focus on?

While starting an organization to raise awareness in your area may be legitimately needed, I wonder if there's another more-needed aspect of anti-trafficking you are uniquely equipped to bring to the table. You may already have some sort of idea what you want to start, but I'd like to stir up your thinking by discussing six unique categories. Even if you think you're not passionate about a specific area, read about it anyway and allow your mind to dream what your "something" could look like. You may be surprised by what comes up for you.

Raising Awareness

Let's begin with the most common focus for those who want to help end human trafficking. It's the easiest way to get involved in the movement, and it's as simple as educating other people on the issue itself. While many people have a cursory view of the problem, there is widespread mis-education on the details of sex trafficking, labor trafficking, and organ trafficking. Therefore, you may want to choose one aspect of trafficking and educate people deeply on that issue.

START SOMETHING TO END TRAFFICKING

For instance, when I started brainstorming my most recent project, I wanted to educate Americans on sex trafficking in the United States and motivate people to take action through the inspiring stories of six female abolitionists. What did I want to accomplish? Educate America on the issue of sex trafficking (not labor or organ), and motivate them to take action in their city. Why? Because many people in the US think that victims are transported into the country from Mexico or Asia, and they don't realize that 80% of victims are US citizens. I wanted people to understand that women and children are being sold in cities across America - including their own area.

If you're interested in raising awareness, consider these questions...

1. **Topic:** What do you want to help people become aware of? Human trafficking in general or sex, labor, or organ trafficking in particular?

2. **Scope:** Are you wanting people to be aware of the presence of the problem in your city, county, state, nation, or our world at large?

3. **Target:** Who do you want to become more aware? Students and teachers at your school, your city, your county, your nation, or the entire world? In other words, who will you be seeking to educate?

4. **Methodology:** How do you want to educate them? Website, classroom curriculum, talks, seminars, events, concerts, films, artwork, guerrilla marketing?

5. **Outcomes:** How will you determine the success of your efforts? # of attenders, amount of money raised for an organization, or particular action taken by people in your target?

Anna, the high school student who raised awareness at her Texas high school, took her campaign to the state level after being chosen as the Director of Activism for the Texas State JSA (Junior State of America). During her senior year, she participated in bringing two human trafficking speakers to state-wide conventions, recruited students to volunteer at organizations, collected signatures for petitions, aligned with the Houston Rescue and Restore Coalition to promote fair trade Starbucks products, and raised money for local non profit organizations. Meanwhile, back at her high school, they decided to create a human trafficking awareness board within their JSA chapter, and it's still in operation now that Anna has graduated.

What Are You Trying to Accomplish?

<u>Decreasing Demand</u>
Another focus of your efforts could be on the "demand" for the services of the person being sold. The reality is there would be no need for the supply if it weren't for the demand. If people would stop buying the product, traffickers would be out of a job.

Notice that this requires a bit more effort and strategy than raising awareness of the issue in a broad manner. Even more intentionality is needed on who to target and how to strategically help them make different choices.

If you're interested in decreasing demand, consider these questions...

1. **Specific Topic:** Decreasing demand of all human trafficking wouldn't be a wise use of your time (in my opinion), and I would suggest you pick a particular aspect - labor, sex, or organ. Unless you have specific contacts in the medical field, my guess is you will want to focus on labor or sex.

2. **Target:** Who do you want to stop making purchases? Male sex buyers in your school, city, county, or nation? Or, business owners in a particular area?

3. **Motivation:** What will you use to motivate buyers to stop purchasing? Educating them on the damage they are causing? Threatening legal action or boycotts? Highlighting or demonstrating the benefits of an alternative?

4. **Methodology:** How do you want to motivate current buyers to choose an alternative? Social media campaign, videos, events, boycotts, petitions, direct conversations, legislation, legal action?

5. **Outcomes:** Will the success of your efforts be based on # of attendees at events, # of arrests, a particular business shut down, or changes in research data?

One such effort that's becoming more popular is what's called a "john school" - an education program for men who have been arrested for purchasing sex. Generally, it's a one-day class where men are given the opportunity for the offense to be expunged from their record by paying a fee and attending the session.

One such program is offered once a month by Kenny Baker, a cognitive behavior therapist who directs The John School in Nashville, Tennessee. Not only does Kenny educate the men on the negative results of high-risk behavior, but he invites Nashville prosecutors to discuss legal ramifications, health department representatives to present about STDs, and several survivors of sex trafficking to share about their experiences. Ultimately, the greatest desire is for the men to deal with the underlying issues that drove them to this point - not just the purchasing of sex itself.

Preventing Human Trafficking
While raising awareness is more focused on a general education and decreasing demand is centered on the buyer, prevention concentrates on the potential victim. Unfortunately, this work is not as popular to entrepreneurial types who are interested in social transformation, because there's no crime or victim involved…yet. When an organization is not stopping or rescuing or restoring, things seem more nebulous, and the outcomes are harder to track. Yet, it is incredibly important.

If you can educate a vulnerable, at-risk individual on how to avoid being coerced or manipulated, you're saving his or her life. If you can open up the possibilities they have for healthy relationships, further education, and expanded job opportunities, you are preventing them from being lured in to the web of traffickers. And, oftentimes, you may find out that someone is already being trafficked or has been trafficked in the past just by educating them on what it is. Many victims don't even realize they've been taken advantage of for the profit and pleasure of others, and you can help connect them to much needed services.

1. **Target:** Who do you want to prevent from being trafficked? At-risk girls (ages 12-17) in your city, county, state, or another country? Immigrants in your city, county, or state? People looking for work in another country?

2. **Methodology:** How do you want to educate them and/or provide alternatives? Flyers, website, school assemblies, juvenile detention program, educational classes, safe job opportunities?

3. **Outcomes:** How will you determine the success of your efforts? # of people warned, # of events, # of new jobs found?

What Are You Trying to Accomplish?

While assisting women to obtain restraining orders through a local domestic violence organization in the early 90's, Jackie Guzman was inspired to provide a "women's empowerment" mentoring program that would bridge opportunities for these women with volunteers. As the lives of women were being transformed, many of them expressed a need to reach and equip their own daughters who were struggling with similar issues.

Founded in 1997, The Glass Slipper (www.theglassslipper.org) provides mentoring and self development programs for at-risk girls, ages 10-18, encouraging transformation from the inside out. As they receive referrals from law enforcement, school districts, social workers, and the community at large, the all-volunteer organization puts on the IMAGE Academy and the IMAGE Boot Camp as well as other programs in order to strengthen girls' self-perception, inspire them to dream big, and make educated choices. In the process, they provide opportunities for the girls to accomplish their goals.

Aftercare for Survivors
One of the most tragic aspects of the movement to end human trafficking is when a victim is rescued, and there are no services available to them to receive aftercare and restoration. Because of their high level of vulnerability, the victim will most likely end up being trafficked soon again, because that's what they know. Although there's abuse and torment involved, they know what to expect, and there's some sense of order or care (as perverted as it may be) they can count on.

In the process of producing the *IN PLAIN SIGHT* documentary, aftercare became a subject of passion for me. To see how women and girls can have their lives healed and restored after experiencing such brutality was an inspiring experience. I've visited five unique aftercare homes, and I've spent quite a bit of time with their founders. These women are extraordinary, and they've been through hell to start these homes and maintain them. It's not glamorous, and it's far from easy to provide a high standard of care.

Opening a home is not something you do overnight (or even within a few months), and it's something that requires hundreds of thousands of dollars - even millions. Property, licensing, programming, trained therapists who specialize in trauma counseling, access to doctors, pro bono attorneys, and direct relationships with law enforcement, FBI, and Homeland Security.

START SOMETHING TO END TRAFFICKING

We need more aftercare homes in the US and around the globe, but we don't need people who have big hearts yet lack strategic planning and expertise. Ultimately, it may do more harm than good.

That's why I love the work of Hope for Justice and their Professional Providers Network. By tapping into the knowledgebase of others and drawing upon the wisdom of those who have walked this road before you, you'll have a much great chance of success.

1. **Survivors:** Who are you wanting to provide aftercare for? Labor trafficking? If so, in your city, county, state, country, or another country? Or, sex trafficking survivors? Adult women, girls, or boys?

2. **Collaboration:** Are you open to helping an existing aftercare home? Would you be open to collaborating with another group that's seeking to start one? Or, do you feel specifically called to start a new home yourself?

3. **Action:** Are you wanting to volunteer your skills or raise money to support an existing aftercare home? Or, are you wanting to get educated and rally a highly-trained team to start the process of opening a home?

To learn more about the five aftercare homes featured in the IN PLAIN SIGHT documentary, I would recommend *Heros of Hope: Intimate Conversations with Six Abolitionists and the Sex Trafficking Survivors They Serve.* (www.bit.ly/HeroesofHope)

Researching the Issue
Gaining a clear picture on the issue (whether sex, labor, or organ) can be one of the most slippery aspects of addressing trafficking. Everyone wants to know, "How big of a problem is this in our community?" Yet, coming up with those numbers can be challenging, and looking at the number of posts on Backpage.com or calculating the # of arrests can be limiting and dissatisfying.

What if you used your training in statistics, research, and even journalism to delve deeper into the issue? What if you were able to provide your school or community or law enforcement or non-profits with a better understanding of what's *really* going on in particular area? Do you think that might be helpful?

What Are You Trying to Accomplish?

1. **Your Focus:** What would you be interested in researching - something about awareness, prevention, rescue, arrests, or aftercare? Examples may include potential # of victims based on a certain vulnerability, holistic picture of available victim services, or determining correlation or causation of a governmental effort.

2. **Research Specificity:** Within the particular research focus, do you want to concentrate specifically on a certain non-profit, city, county, states, or country?

3. **Outcomes:** What will you do with your findings? How will you leverage, publicize, or integrate the information?

When Rachel Sparks heard about the issue of child prostitution, she rallied a small film crew and set out to research and expose the issue in the nation of Thailand. As they interviewed prostitute after prostitute, they heard a common thread that pointed to the initial state of vulnerability - poverty, a lack of education, and a lack of options. The team soon met Cat, then 10 years old, living in poverty with her mother (a former prostitute) who worked tirelessly so she could afford to keep her daughter in school. Cat's education was soon to become too expensive, and her mother's health was failing. Cat would soon have to go to the city to work even though it would only cost about a dollar a day to keep her in school and out of the city.

When Rachel and her team returned to the US and screened a rough cut of the documentary featuring Cat's story, family and friends wanted to know if there were other children like Cat who needed help to stay in school. The SOLD Project (www.thesoldproject.com) was born and scholarship funds were established for other at-risk children in Cat's village.

Over five years later and now under the leadership of Rachel Goble, The SOLD Project has significantly expanded their work to help educate children - teaching them to avoid exploitation and guiding them on a path to success.

They know from previous research that their program has successfully decreased school dropout rates from 50% to less than 10%, but they are ready to embark on a more extensive research project to learn just why their programs are working so well. As you can imagine, the ultimate desire is to replicate the success in more locations.

START SOMETHING TO END TRAFFICKING

Starting a Business

Envisioning, launching, and operating a business that is run with integrity, provides a solid product/service, and benefits the community at large is a powerful way to help end human trafficking in our world. Whether you're using the business to raise money for a non-profit or you're actually providing fair-paying jobs for survivors, you are contributing to the movement.

While giving 10% of proceeds and simultaneously raising awareness is helpful at some level, I would challenge you to think more creatively about how you can leverage the power of a business. One of the greatest problems that non-profits have is sustaining income from their donor base. If non-profits could partner with entrepreneurs to create sustainable businesses whose purpose is to fund the work of the non-profit, I'm wondering if these organizations would struggle less through the ups and downs of the economy. The challenge, of course, is to avoid distracting or depleting the resources of the non-profit in the process of starting the business.

As an entrepreneur, you have the ability to create something that is truly beneficial to everyone involved - employees, buyers, community at large, non-profit, and survivors.

1. **Type of Business:** Are you wanting to sell a product made by yourself, survivors, or someone else? Do you want to offer it online or at home parties, flea markets, boutiques, or mass retail?

2. **Buyers:** Do you have a community of people who are already interested in the products or the cause? Is it your school, church, non-profit supporters, or social media contacts?

3. **Profits:** What will you do with profits? Donate to a non-profit, support the hiring and employing of survivors, or invest in the start of a new endeavor?

Since he was a young boy, Nick Elcock had a love for sandals, and he wondered if he might start a sandal company one day in the distant future. After becoming aware of the issue of sex trafficking, he began to envision a creative way to support the work of Courage Worldwide, an aftercare home based in northern California for children rescued from sex trafficking.

In 2014, Sovereign Sandals (www.sovereignsandals.com) launched it's first line of artisan sandals, handmade in California, utilizing high quali-

What Are You Trying to Accomplish?

ty, locally-sourced materials. The Sovereign woven label was intentionally placed on the left sandal, the same side as the human heart, representative of the compassion the buyer demonstrates from each Sovereign purchase. With each pair of sandals sold, Sovereign donates a percentage of their profits to help further the work of Courage Worldwide.

What Do You Bring to the Table?
Now that I've stretched your mind to think about these six ways you can be involved in helping to end human trafficking, I want to help you begin to narrow down your efforts through a few questions. Don't rush through the process. Feel free to put the book down, reflect on the questions, ask a friend what they think, and come back to it. Grab a pen, fill in the blanks, and write in the margins.

1. **What area of human trafficking are you most passionate about?**

    - ❏ **Awareness** - helping people become aware of human trafficking.
    - ❏ **Demand** - decreasing the purchase or use of human beings.
    - ❏ **Prevention** - stopping people from being enslaved.
    - ❏ **Aftercare** - restoring survivors of trafficking.
    - ❏ **Research** - understanding more about the issue.
    - ❏ **Business** - creating a business that has responsible practices.

2. **What unique talents, skills, or experiences do you have?**

    Think for a moment about what you bring to the table. Are you a natural leader or super organized or incredibly creative? People probably say, "Wow, you're really good at that." That's something unique you can bring to this movement. What is it?

    _____
    _____
    _____
    _____

3. **What resources can you utilize?**

    All of us have resources at our disposal. What are yours? Do you have available time to invest? Do you have a large group of friends or an organization/church you can rally? Do you have money to leverage toward your efforts? What about an extra vehicle, property, or office you have access to? Think broadly about your resources.

START SOMETHING TO END TRAFFICKING

_____
_____
_____
_____

4. How much time and energy do you want to invest?

While you may have the best intentions in the world, you also need to be realistic about what you can invest in what you're starting. Do you envision this as a one-week project or an organization that will last for years or something in between? And, how many hours per week can you invest in this effort at what level of energy?

Length of investment: _____ weeks _____ months _____ years

Hours per week: _____ Level of energy: high   mid   low

Now that you're beginning to identify your passion and what you have to bring to the table, let's put it all together to get a clearer picture.

_____ + _____ +
your area of passion (one of the six)   your talent, skill, & experience

_____ + _____ =
your resources   time & energy to invest

While this is in no way an exact formula, it's designed to help you become aware of what you're bringing to the table. You may have hit upon a new area of human trafficking you'd like to address, and you may be more aware of what you're able or willing to invest.

If you have a vision to start a global organization to reduce demand but only have a couple of hours to invest every week, you may want to rethink what you can accomplish. If you were thinking you'd like to raise the awareness of your school but have a degree in research with quite a few hours available to invest, you may want to examine how you could leverage your educational experience in a different way.

What Are You Trying to Accomplish?

Before we move forward, let me remind you of the truths we talked about in the Introduction as well as the "whys" you identified in Chapter One.

As we begin to get specific about opportunities in front of you, you might start to hear the whisper of lies such as *"you can't do this, you're not enough, or people won't support you."* Don't believe that junk. You're ready for this. You were made for this moment. Keep going and remember your "whys"...

- Human beings are inherently valuable and have equal worth.
- No person should ever be bought or sold.
- Coercion, manipulation, abuse, and violence are intolerable.
- All three parties involved are in need of restoration.
- Human trafficking can be prevented.
- Each one of us has a role to play to prevent and end tr**afficking.**

Let's Get Clear About Your Vision.
Although you'll continue to refine what you're trying to accomplish as you move forward, I want to help you choose your "something" (what you want to start) so we can use it as a working example throughout the rest of the book.

If you're the type of person who doesn't want to make a choice because you feel like you're limiting your future options, please know that you can always change your mind, make shifts, or add something to the mix. I just want to help you walk through the process so that you know how to get clear and what your next steps can be.

I want to start a _____ that will _____
               project, event, campaign, organization

_____
                   who and how will it help?

with the goal of _____.
                  what is your desired outcome?

We'll focus on the *how* and *when* in the next chapters, but for now, I just want you to be able to say, "This is what I'm starting. Here's what I'm passionate about doing, and here is the outcome or goal that I'm shooting for."

Got it?

START SOMETHING TO END TRAFFICKING

Okay, now I want you to take a moment and envision what it's going to be like when this "something" comes to fruition. Close your eyes and imagine this project, event, campaign, or organization is in full swing. Everything is going beautifully - just as your had desired.

What do you see? Get ready to close your eyes.

What do you feel? Excitement, thankfulness, energetic, hopeful?

Who do you see working alongside you? Friends, family, new people?

What else do you notice? Anything surprise you? Any warning signs to be aware of?

If you haven't already, close your eyes, and allow the picture of your "something" to take shape in your mind's eye. Allow it to unfold in full color with sights, smells, and textures.

Our mind is a powerful tool, and by envisioning what we long to experience, it can create internal motivation to propel us forward. Anytime I'm thinking about a new project, I visualize the fulfillment of the dream. I see the documentary completely finished before I even begin. I see people sitting in a packed theatre as their minds are opened up to the reality of trafficking. I imagine myself walking into a bookstore and seeing the dvd, cd, and book displayed together on the endcap, and I see people purchasing them as a tool for both education and motivation.

This visualization is a powerful tool that motivates me when I'm tired or overwhelmed. It takes me back to my vision and reminds me what I'm trying to accomplish.

Can you see your "something" clearly yet?

Chapter Three
HOW TO LAUNCH A PROJECT

As a mom of four kids living in Eden Prairie, Minnesota, Christine Erickson had plenty on her plate, but she found herself desiring something more. As a follower of Jesus, she began to pray, "God, break my heart for the things that make your heart break," and the answer came a few months later as her heart was broken for girls and women trapped in sex trafficking.

In an effort to bring awareness to the sexual exploitation of youth in her surrounding communities, she envisioned and organized a 5k walk/run called "Stop the Trafficking" (www.stopthetraffickingrun.org), and 850 people participated. Over $18,000 was raised and donated to four local organizations that provide housing and programming for trafficked youth. They're already planning next year's event and anticipating over 1,000 people to participate.

Starting Projects, Events, Campaigns, and Organizations
For the sake of our conversation, I've chosen to break down your possible "something" into four categories in order to help create boundaries for our discussion. In this case, a "project" is anything that's not an event, not a fundraising campaign, and not an organization. Is there overlap? Of course. Some projects have fundraising involved, and some will include an event. Examples of "projects" may include...

- Recording a music album to raise awareness.
- Creating a podcast to interview key anti-trafficking leaders.
- Researching the connection of local adult stores to trafficking.
- Launching a volunteer recruitment effort for an aftercare home.
- Starting an afterschool education program for at-risk girls.

START SOMETHING TO END TRAFFICKING

I've set apart specific chapters on events, campaigns, and organizations, because of the unique questions that must be addressed in the process. Yet, there are many things you may want to start that don't fit into those three categories, and I'd like to share the general process I go through on each and every project I take on.

Who Will You Work With?
Prior to starting any project, I am keenly aware of who I'm working with. It has taken me years to understand that I like to work alone. As I write this, I'm sitting in the front seat of my truck in the parking lot of the Newport Beach pier, and you can find me here (or my kitchen table) on most days. I have set up my life to be able to work with a phone, a laptop, and Wi-Fi - in silence. I have meetings several times a week, but I prefer talking on the phone than meeting in person. It works for me. I thrive in that environment, and people hire me to get things done because I've figured this out.

I like to be hired by people who are starting their own projects.
I like to start my own projects and collaborate with and hire others.
I'm not fond of partnering with other people.

Even though I have a long-term friend as a business partner on a project right now, I've learned to avoid it. The process of developing a partnership, working through all the kinks, and seeing the project come to fruition has not worked well for me. I like to take direction or give direction...but that's just me. You have to figure out your best-case working practices on your own.

As you consider working with others, here are several things to consider...

- **Option #1:** This is your project, and you'll collaborate with other people and organizations to complete it.

- **Option #2:** This is someone else's project, and you are going to help them complete it.

- **Option #3:** You are equally partnering with another person on the project, and you're both responsible for co-leading and completion.

I would caution you on starting any project without an understanding of who is leading the effort. If you have a group of friends who think you'll all just sing Kumbayah and make everything work smoothly, my guess is that someone is going to throw a wrench in your "something" along the way. Because of the importance of working with others, I've dedicated an entire chapter to raising up leaders, rallying volunteers, and how to work with others in order to start your "something". (Chapter Seven)

Trust Is Everything
No matter what you're starting (project, event, campaign, or organization), trust is absolutely everything. It can take years to build a solid base of trust with people, but it can only take a matter of moments to lose it.

When starting a project, the only way that people or organizations will be willing to work with you is if they trust you. Things that build trust include...

- Your reputation in your community.
- Your track record of performance.
- Showing up to appointments on time.
- Responding to communication (email or phone) in a timely manner.
- Using professional language.
- Caring for a person (not just your project).
- Speaking kindly of others who are not in your presence.
- Creating quality communication materials that represent your project in a professional manner (graphics, website, social media, etc.)

If people trust that your "yes" means "yes" and your "no" means "no", they'll be more likely to help you. This isn't just a tactical strategic issue; this is a character issue. I've gained the trust of thousands along the way, and I've also lost it at points by not living out each of the above. Find ways to build trust - not because it will help you launch a successful project, but because it's a reflection of your character.

Seven Powerful Questions
As I'm thinking about any possible project, I generally start by "big boarding" possible ideas connected to the effort. If I'm working alone, I'll type out all my thoughts on my laptop (usually in "Things" - a Mac-based to-do list) so that I can edit it as I refine my ideas. If I'm working with others, we'll usually gather around a large pad of paper on an easel and capture everyone's ideas.

Here are the questions I ask for every single project...

START SOMETHING TO END TRAFFICKING

- What is the desired outcome?
- Who will this impact or benefit?
- Who can we learn from?
- What are the major steps we need to take?
- When do these steps need to be completed?
- What is this going to cost us?
- Who is going to do what?

Let's take the IN PLAIN SIGHT benefit music album as a sample project (www.bit.ly/IPSbenefitalbum) to run through these questions. These were our answers last year when we were brainstorming about this project.

- **What is the desired outcome?**
  We want to raise money for Hope for Justice through a music album while simultaneously creating a broader resource offering when the documentary and devotional are made available.

- **Who will this impact or benefit?**
  This will financially benefit the work of Hope for Justice, and it will give buyers an action step. They will have a sense of participation in the cause, and they will enjoy the inspiring music. This will also give a music artist and their label the opportunity to participate in the cause in an easy way.

- **Who can we learn from?**
  International Justice Mission has done similar projects. Let's check with the Executive Producer of their most recent project.

- **What are the major steps we need to take?**
  - Ask Word Entertainment if they will distribute the CD.
  - Announce CD project to supporters via email and social media.
  - Hire an Executive Producer to acquire the song rights.
  - Write an introductory explanation letter to music labels.
  - Contact labels to seek the song rights.
  - Design the CD packaging.
  - Create and implement a marketing plan.

- **When do these steps need to be completed?**
  We'll need to determine the timeline after speaking with Word.

How to Launch a PROJECT

- **What is this going to cost us?**
  We will be able to determine the cost of the project in the process of bringing on an Executive Producer - his/her time, licensing fees, manufacturing, marketing, etc.

- **Who is going to do what?**
  David will contact a possible Executive Producer. If hired, they will determine who will take on each of the tasks.

In the beginning, Word Entertainment said "yes" to distributing the album, and Randy Williams (from Big Tent Revival) agreed to join the project as Executive Producer. Unfortunately, due to the fact that this is a benefit album, Word's legal department eventually said "no" to distribution, but they helped make an introduction to a nationwide chain of Christian bookstores. Awaken Media (the non-profit I lead) set up a 90 day exclusive, and we were able to communicate this to labels in order to help them feel secure about the project. Once we had the release date, we were able to set deadlines for all the other aspects of the project.

Things changed along the way, but the seven questions constantly drove the process. These are the questions that I ask clients when I consult them on marketing projects, and these are the questions I ask myself. They're simple, yet powerful.

Although each of the questions is important, I especially want to encourage you to consider who you can learn from. Most likely, you're not the first to do what you're doing. Your "something" will definitely be unique in some way, but there are others who have walked this road before you.

Has someone written articles or books on the subject? Have you searched online for similar projects? Have you contacted the person or organization who is behind it? Have you emailed or called them to ask as many questions as you can think of? The education you will gain from others who have done it before you has the potential to save you an enormous amount of time and money.

Asking For Permission (or Forgiveness)
Although I feel quite self-empowered to start something anytime I like, I've also found out the hard way that permission is often needed. Can you imagine if we wanted to raise money and never asked the music label if we could use an artist's song? Can you say "cease and desist" and "lawsuit"?

Great wisdom is required in knowing whether permission is required or if it's better to ask for forgiveness later.

First of all, is anything a potential legal issue? If you are using someone else's physical or intellectual property (music, film, imagery, words, etc.), you need permission (in writing). Are you using a name that has been trademarked? (I've had to rename a book because of this issue, and on a separate occasion, I lost a $2,000 investment on an iPhone app - both trademark issues.) For more information, visit www.uspto.gov/trademarks.

If you are part of an existing organization, do you need permission from the leaders to start this project? If it's going to be an official project of the organization, absolutely yes. If it's something you're doing on your own, it would be wise to give them a heads up and seek their blessing. If it's not an official project within the organization but you're rallying volunteers (and possibly donors) to help with your project, you're looking for trouble. Honor the leadership of the organization and discuss your ideas and intentions.

Finally, if it's not a legal or organizational issue, would it be beneficial to your relationship with a person or organization to get their permission, blessing, or involvement? Don't unnecessarily step on someone's toes just because you're excited about the project you're launching. Other organizations may have been working on something similar or in a similar geographical area and developing a relationship (not necessarily seeking permission) would be extremely wise.

Years ago when pastoring a church, I had the idea of starting a ministry to a particular street in challenged area of town. We hosted a backpack giveaway to help families with school supplies, we hosted fun street parties, and we even announced free rides on our graphics-wrapped bus to church. Let's just say that another organization who had been working in that neighborhood *for years* wasn't very thrilled that we just barged in and started announcing all these things. Did we need their permission? No. Would a conversation to seek to understand the community and this organization's strategy been helpful? Extremely. I would have launched that project in a completely different way with what I know now.

Best and Worst Case Scenarios
There are two additional questions that I start to turn over in my mind as a project is coming into focus...

How to Launch a PROJECT

- **What if this works well beyond expectations? (best case)**
- **What if this goes really bad? (worst case)**

The first question prepares you for the onslaught of more participants, more sales, more information, more _____. We always seem to want more of everything, but sometimes more can be a problem. If this thing *actually* works, you may be hard-pressed to handle the surge if you don't have a back-up plan.

Let's take the example of the benefit music album. What if we have too many artists who want to donate songs? We could choose the ones who will be the best fit for the project. What if all the CDs sell out of the retail stores in the first month? We can simply manufacture more and have them shipped to the chain's distribution center immediately. What if more retail chains call before the 90 day exclusive with the first chain is up? We can ask for a purchase order and prepare for another marketing push.

Now, what about the worst case scenarios? What if things go really bad? Beyond helping me mitigate potential losses, I often use this question as a way to quiet the anxiety in my heart if I'm stressed out about a project. Yes, it's helpful as a pre-planning mechanism, but it's often a strategy to help me see that the worst-case scenario isn't *that* bad.

Back to the music album and questions I mulled over last year prior to the project. What if none of the record labels we plan to approach will let their artist's songs be used for the album? We could keep looking until we find labels or independent artists who want to participate. What if the licensing agreements take longer than expected? We could push back the release date. What if very few of the CDs sell and little money is raised? We can't control the outcome, and maybe we'll be selling them at the local swap meet. (I hope not.)

The worst-case scenario also gives you the opportunity to be reminded of the list of resources that are setting you up to win. In our case with the album, I was reminded of our relationship with Word Entertainment to help us think through any challenging issues, our support from Hope for Justice who is the financial beneficiary, a wide network of artists that our Executive Producer knows, and the ability to go to other retail chains if the first relationship didn't work out for some reason. Lots of support and possible solutions are what I like to see.

START SOMETHING TO END TRAFFICKING

The Excitement of the Beginning

I love everything about the beginning of a project. The dreaming, the brainstorming, the list making - all of it creates energy within my mind and body, and I'm fired up to get going. Three of the most common things that I find myself focusing on are...

- **Research**

  Do as much research as possible in the beginning so that you're prepared to answer questions from potential supporting organizations, fellow leaders, and volunteers. Although it's okay to say "I'm not sure" and "I need to look into that", the more you are prepared to have a solid answer - the better. Research also helps you avoid potential, upcoming landmines and helps you foresee opportunities that you could miss if you weren't aware of the possibilities.

  In the case of the benefit album, we discovered early on that a compilation of hymns would be the easiest option because the songs are public domain (due to age). That would mean we wouldn't have to get licensing rights from the company who owned the song itself - just from the label who owned the recording of the song. Huge difference.

- **Questions and answers**

  In the beginning of almost every project, you'd be wise to ask as many questions as possible. Anytime a question pops into your head, write it down if you don't know the answer. Then, ask yourself, "Who is most equipped to answer this question?" Get in touch with them, and get the best answer possible. If you can't know the answer until a certain time in the future or until something else happens first, don't misplace that question. Keep it somewhere. You need to know the answer.

- **Listmaking**

  I'm a list maker. The more it's down on paper (or computer), the less anxiety I feel. I want to know that I've thought about what I need to do, and I've put a deadline of some sort next to it (today, tomorrow, a date, or reminder for the future). In a moment, I'll share with you the basic process I use to manage daily progress, but I've found that I make more lists in the beginning part of a project than in the middle or latter stages.

How to Launch a PROJECT

Pain in the Middle

The middle of any project can be the most challenging for me. I get frustrated with inevitable delays caused by someone not getting back to me or the bureaucracy of an organization. This is also right about the time when I realize the project has creeped beyond its initial scope, and I'm feeling like I've bit off a bit more than I can chew.

There's a 99.9% chance that I'm going to say, "Wow, this is quite a bit more difficult than I anticipated", and my wife is going to roll her eyes and respond with, "That's what you say every time!"

It's true. In the beginning of almost every single project, I'm fired up with excitement, but I underestimate the amount of blood, sweat, and tears that its going to take. I don't know if I'm short-sighted, blinded by my love for the project, or it's the Universe's way of roping me into something that I might otherwise say no to.

When I first came up with the idea of the documentary on sex trafficking in the US, that's all it was...a documentary. Somehow, a benefit music album was added on...and then a devotional/study guide. Three resources were planned, and they were set to be released on the same day.

"Hmmm, wouldn't it be helpful if the interviews from the documentary were transcribed and put into a book?" I thought to myself. Within days, I had the audio files being transcribed, and I was in the process of designing the cover. That project alone took over 50 hours for me to manage the transcription, design the cover and interior, edit every interview for readability, write an introduction for the book and for each interview, edit the interviewee's photo for their chapter, and on and on. That single good idea caused me a great deal of pain in the middle of the project.

The only way I was able to finish that book project (or any project for that matter) was to re-align my mind and heart with the vision.

"Yes, this is painful. Yes, this is more work than I imagined or dreamed. Why am I doing this? Because I want people who are passionate about anti-trafficking to have these 14 interviews as a resource. I want people to be able to read the full interview in context and not just hear a snippet in the film. I want these stories to be heard, because I believe more people will be motivated to take action."

Notice the question, "Why am I doing this?" Two reasons - the ultimate "whys" we talked about in Chapter One and the clear vision you articulated in Chapter Two. Without either of those things, you're likely to lose momentum and perhaps even quit when it gets painful in the middle. While I'm having this conversation with myself (usually in bed while I'm tossing and turning), I'm envisioning someone holding the book, reading it, and being inspired and motivated. Reminding myself and anyone I'm working with about the vision, the reason why we're working so hard, and the ultimate desired outcome is the much-needed boost of energy that everyone needs. A clear vision is what allows all of us to press on and overcome obstacles.

Finishing Strong
You don't want to be so sick of the project that you're just thankful to be done or so tired that you're stumbling over the finish line. You want to leave enough steam to push hard through the finish to do the following...

- **Complete and launch**
  Whatever the project is, complete it. Don't leave a couple of things hanging out there. Do what you said you were going to do, and launch it out there for the world to experience (whoever it is you intended it to impact or benefit).

- **Communicate the wins**
  Don't just quietly complete the project and walk away. Who needs to learn about it? In the case of a benefit album, thousands will hear about it (and hopefully buy it for the benefit of Hope for Justice), but some projects are more behind the scenes. Would a press release be helpful (which we'll discuss in a later chapter)? Or, is it as simple as an email to supporters, a phone call to an organization leader, or an announcement at an upcoming meeting? Be sure to share what went well and how the project is going or how it made a difference.

- **Learnings and next steps**
  Either by yourself or with your team, take time to reflect on what could have gone better. In my experience, something can always be done even better in order to experience an even greater outcome. I like to see it, take note, and think about how to integrate that in the future. In addition, you'll want to ask yourself and others, "What's the next step?" Do you need to keep going with the project, transition the project to a new leader, or consider it completed?

How to Launch a PROJECT

Throughout all three points of a project (beginning, middle, and end), I'm generally thinking about making daily progress, managing expectations, communicating constantly, and managing money. While these four learned skills are pertinent to anything you are starting, let's take a few minutes to address them in the context of a project.

Making Daily Progress
For better or worse, I tend to measure the quality of my day based on what I accomplished. It's the way I'm wired, but I've also developed some mechanisms that accentuate my ability to get things done...

- **I live by my to-do list.**
  As I mentioned before, I use Things (a Mac-based to-do list software) on my laptop, and I'm constantly updating it. Checking things off my list as complete gives me great satisfaction. Even to the point that if I complete a task I wasn't planning on (such as running to the post office), I'll take two seconds to type it as a task and check it off as complete. Ahhhhh. Can you feel the satisfaction? I can. Things allows me to organize my to-do's by project and by time due.

- **I review my to-do list in the afternoon or evening.**
  Before I go to bed, I already know what I'll be tackling the next day. I don't wait until the morning to think, "Hmm...what should I do today?" I wake up with energy in my step, because I've already been thinking about what I want to accomplish.

- **I motivate myself with my "whys" and a clear vision.**
  Why do I have the energy to do so much? I attribute it to two things - my "whys" and a clear vision for anything that lands on my to-do list. I want to have a definitive reason why I do everything. If something isn't driven by the deepest "whys" in my life or a vision to accomplish it, it's probably not going on my list.

- **I constantly ask myself, "What's next?"**
  Transitioning from one task to the next can be a possible lag point in my day. I'm prone to head on over to the giant time-suck of Facebook and scroll, scroll, scroll as I look for something that will give me a hit of adrenaline. By asking "what's next?", I'm prompting my brain to kick into gear and jump right into the next task on my to-do list. I ask the question when I go to the bathroom, after I get off a phone call, when I'm done sending an email, after returning from an

errand. I'm constantly asking, "what's next?"

- **I get a lot of rest and sleep.**
  Because I have my own business(es), I have the opportunity to set my own schedule, which often means that I'm wrapping things up around 3 or 4pm. After 3ish, I don't schedule important meetings or any creative heavy lifting, because I know that I'm not going to be at my best. I am most creative and productive from 6am-3pm. After that, I find that connecting with my family, doing non-stressful administrative tasks, or resting are best for me. I give my brain an opportunity to rest, and I definitely get 8-9 hours of sleep every night. If I have a big deadline, I'll go to bed at 8pm and get up at 5am to start working on it. Sleep is one of my most powerful secret weapons that helps me get things done.

Managing Expectations

Throughout any project, you have the opportunity to manage your own expectations as well as the expectations of others. We all have expectations... over everything and everyone. I can vacillate from super-high expectations of myself and others ("This has to be the best thing ever.") to incredibly low expectations of the project ("This thing is falling apart.") I am constantly evaluating my expectations and bringing them back to a point that feels more realistic. A great deal of this is happening in the self-talk realm as I go about my daily tasks...

Pressure: "I've gotta make this the best thing ever. It has to succeed."

Response: "I'm doing the best that I can with the resources I have available, and I'm trusting God with the results as I continue to work hard."

As I'm evaluating and managing my own expectations, I also take the time to do that with and for others. By keeping others aware of the status of the project, I manage what they're expecting. Whether it's the content of the project, the timing of it's completion, how much it's costing, or the quality of the project, people you are working with - leaders, volunteers, organizations, customers - all have expectations. You want to meet or exceed those expectations, and that requires you to update them along the way.

Communicating Constantly

There are many forms of communication in our world today - face to face, phone calls, emails, texts, and direct messaging on social media. While I'll

How to Launch a PROJECT

address when and how to use these tools in an upcoming chapter, you'll want to take advantage of all of them as you start your project.

In the past, I had a boss challenge our team to "over-communicate" during the most stressful times of a project. In other words, don't just assume that the other person knows what you're thinking or planning. If you don't communicate, people may feel left out, isolated, and eventually disengage. People want to know what's going on and how they can be part of the effort.

Be explicit, and give regular updates so that people feel included in the process. If there are major changes, sit down face to face or make that phone call. Don't procrastinate, because you're worried about their reaction. Deal with it sooner than later so that you can resolve any challenges and move on with the project.

Managing Money
On rare occasions, money isn't involved, but most projects require some form of financial fuel to get off the ground. When someone other than you is providing the finances, thank them appropriately, update them regularly, and celebrate the completion in a personal way. Without their money, you wouldn't be launching the project.

Whether it's someone else's money or your own, manage it well. Whenever I spend money on a project, I ask myself, "Will this financial investment help us successfully complete the project? Is the return on investment worth spending the money?"

One option I considered for the benefit album was hiring a house band in Nashville and asking every artist to come in and record a new hymn for the album. All the songs would have been brand new and never before released recordings. After calculating that investment, it became clear that approaching labels for donated songs would be much more effective in the long run.

I also knew the CD had a significantly higher chance of timely completion if I hired an Executive Producer to work on the project - rather than me personally tracking down all those labels on my own. We needed someone who had relationships with these labels and knew how to "talk the talk." The financial investment to hire him was well worth it, and I was able to complete the project without a huge headache or stress on my part.

START SOMETHING TO END TRAFFICKING

Although your project will be different, you'll be confronted with opportunities to invest financial resources in multiple directions in order to complete the project. Use the money as the gift that it is, but use it well.

Nourishing Survivors Through the Power of Food
After living for 6 months on a humanitarian ship in Fiji, working at a dental clinic in Haiti, and teaching English in Ethiopia, Keturah Schroeder spent three years working with an international anti-human trafficking organization.

"I knew the stats, the figures, the systemic causes, where it was most prolific, the complexities of supply chains, and more. Without batting an eye, I could tell you that human trafficking is the fastest growing criminal industry in the world, generating more than $32 billion a year - $10 billion of which is generated in the US. Compared to the average person, I thought I was an expert in human trafficking."

In the process, Keturah felt like she was talking theoretically more than living it out. It wasn't until she returned to her home state of Ohio that she discovered Freedom a la Cart, a catering business and workforce development program that prepares local, adult survivors of human trafficking for economic self-sufficiency.

"For the first time in my life, I am working with survivors day in and day out, *and* actually fighting human trafficking. I am working with an incredible organization that is practicing daily what they preach."

Since 2011, Freedom a la Cart (www.freedomalacart.org) has educated thousands of community members, and doubled revenue each year. The survivors cater weddings, dinner parties at the Governor's Residence, and many high-profile women's initiative events. In the last two years, they have employed 25 survivors and provided supportive services to 75 other survivors.

Chapter Four
HOW TO HOST AN EVENT

Envisioning, planning, and putting on an event is a great deal of work, but the results can be tremendous in our fight to end human trafficking. There's no better way to move a group of people toward action than to gather them all in the same room and help them experience something together that they could never experience on their own.

When I was a pastor, I helped plan, create, and host literally hundreds of events, and I love it! The possibilities are endless, and that's why it's all the more important to ask yourself key questions from the very start. After walking you through the basic questions I address before planning any experience, then we'll look at a critical checklist of items that you'll want to think through before your upcoming event.

Key Questions in Planning an Event
As you're probably coming to find out, questions are the key to everything when you're starting your "something." They cause you to think about things you wouldn't normally think of. They slow down your excited process to force you to consider things that will make your event an experience that guests will be talking about for months or days to come.

- **What are the desired outcomes?**
  The most important question of all, "What are you trying to achieve with this event?" It drives everything you'll be planning. Are you seeking to educate people on the subject of trafficking, motivate them to take action in a specific way, raise money for a particular project or non-profit, or create synergy among a group of people?

START SOMETHING TO END TRAFFICKING

Prior to the release of the IN PLAIN SIGHT documentary, we held 16 premieres around the nation, and the organizations featured in the film hosted all of them except one. I wanted to host one in Orange County, California, where I live, since I have so many contacts in the area who know what I've been working on at a national level. My desired outcome was to educate people in my area on the issue of sex trafficking and motivate several key leaders to host film screenings in their neighboring communities a few months later.

By stating what my desired outcome is, I'm simultaneously eliminating a long list of other possible results. I wasn't trying to raise $100,000 or have 100 volunteers sign up. I was raising awareness and rallying people to host screenings. That was the purpose. If you try to do too many things at one time, your core message can get lost among multiple points of communication.

- **Who should be in the room?**
  In order to experience a desired outcome, there is a certain group of people who will need to be "in the room". In other words, who should be on the invite list in order to achieve this result? You may end up casting the net far and wide to invite everyone, but there will probably be a key group of people you definitely want to be there. Who are they? Make the list.

- **What will motivate them to attend?**
  The success of achieving your desired outcome is directly dependent on the attendance of the "right" people and ultimately what they experience. Before we can have them experience the event, we have to incentivize them to attend. Is it the intrigue of wanting to learn more? Is it a concern for their local community? Is it a desire to personally support you and your passions? Is it an opportunity to meet people they've been wanting to connect with? Is it a fun experience with food and drinks? What is it? What's going to motivate them to set aside time from their normal schedule and give you a few hours of their attention?

- **What will this group of people experience together?**
  Not only do you need the right people in the room to reach your desired outcome, but you'll need a program that resonates with your audience and propels them toward that outcome. The "experience" begins the moment they hear about the event and continues on until

they walk out of the venue at the end of the occasion. In fact, you'll probably even want to extend their experience through a follow-up contact, informational recap, or online connection. All of these touch points will add up to their holistic experience.

Coffee With a Cause
As Stephanie Strauss opened a new CD by Natalie Grant, she had no idea that her life was about to be changed. As she read the liner notes from her home in Middletown, Pennsylvania, her mind was awakened to the tragedy of human trafficking around the globe.

"Looking the other way was not an option for me. Around this same time, I needed a service project for National Honor Society as a junior in high school and the PUREhope Coffeehouse was born."

Six years ago at the age of 17, Stephanie started what has turned into a yearly fundraiser for Hope for Justice. Held in a social hall at her church, the event includes local musicians, fresh baked goods, fair trade, organic coffee, and items for a silent auction - all donated by local businesses. People make a donation of $5 for bottomless beverages or a $10 donation and receive a PUREhope mug and bottomless beverages.

With a clear desired outcome (raising awareness and money), Stephanie has found the right combination of coffee and entertainment to motivate people in her area to attend. At the first event in 2009, she raised $750 with 30 people in attendance, and the event has grown year after year - raising over $2,700 in 2014 with over 100 people at the event.

22 Critical Steps to a Successful Event
As I begin the planning process for any event, I begin to work my way through the following checklist to ensure success. The plans that result can't be centered on my own personal style or preferences; it's all about motivating the people who will be in attendance and ultimately reaching the desired outcome.

1. **Find the Best Location.**
   In order to attract the right audience and reach your desired outcome, where should this event be held? It may be tempting to automatically opt for a venue you're comfortable with such as your church or school, but I want to challenge you to think outside that literal box. Is there another location in your community even better?

For a decade, I pastored churches that were "portable" - meaning, we didn't have our own facility. We met in school auditoriums or community centers on Sundays, and all our other events were held in homes or different venues in the community. While other pastors were opting to hold everything at their church building, we had the privilege (and challenge) of finding new locations for events on a regular basis.

Some people aren't comfortable going to a church or a university. What about a community center, performing arts venue, the home of a wealthy friend, a gymnasium, a local park, a theatre, or an underground parking garage? I can turn any venue into an event location, but the more the location resonates with the desired outcome *and* the attendees - the better.

2. Choose an Attractive Day and Time.
What is the optimal day and time to have the right people in attendance? Depending on the nature of the event, most people need 3-4 weeks to put something on their calendar. If it's a large event, you'll want to give people 3-4 months to ensure they'll be available. Is the date open at the proposed venue? Are there any holidays that may distract people from attending? Will most people be in town during that time (versus on vacation)? Is there a major cultural event on television that will decrease your attendance? Does the starting time of the event give people enough margin to get off work, pick up their kids, have dinner, etc.? And, does the ending time give people enough space to get other things accomplished in their day or evening?

3. Provide Sufficient Parking.
Unless your event is being held for students on a college campus or for residents who are used to taking public transportation, most people will be driving to your event, and they'll need a place to park. Does the invitation need to tell them where to park? Is parking close to the entrance? Is there handicap parking? Will they have to pay to park? Are you telling them this information upfront, or are *you* paying for the parking in advance? Is the parking well-lit and safe if you're hosting a night-time event? Is it in an area where a security guard should be hired to patrol the parking lot during the event? Would it be helpful to have volunteers waving people into the venue and helping them park?

How to Host an EVENT

4. Arrange Adequate Seating.
Does the venue have adequate seating for those in attendance? Whether you're hosting a film screening, a multi-course dinner, or a dance party, people want to sit down. Older theatres have seats built for the butt-width and knee-length of a small child. What about handicap access and seating? Is the venue accessible to someone who is using a wheelchair or walker?

Can you change the arrangement of the seating? A church filled with forward-facing pews creates a different experience than an open room with chairs arranged in a half-circle versus round tables surrounded by six to eight chairs each. How will your seating help or hurt your desired outcome (and the butts of those in attendance)?

5. Design a Compelling Invitation.
Although we'll spend an entire chapter on communications and marketing, I just want to remind you of the importance of the invitation. It must compel and attract people to the event. Be clear about the name of the event, date, time, location, and the reason why someone would want to attend. You're not just thinking about *your* agenda. You are thinking about *theirs*. What will attract the invitee to want to attend?

Because of the nature of the subject, would it be helpful to put an age suggestion or a notation about what will be discussed? *"Parents: Human trafficking is a challenging subject, and information that is presented may not be appropriate for children."*

Many parents will want a specific cut off age, but that can be different for each child and each event. In the case of the IN PLAIN SIGHT documentary, we tell parents that the film is about sex trafficking and therefore discusses adult material. Although we don't sexualize the subject or recreate any scenes, abolitionists and survivors share their raw, personal experiences. If the child knows about sex and can handle an adult conversation about sex, violence, and the recovery process, then it would be appropriate for them.

6. Invite Important Guests.
Every attendee is important, but there are some people you want to make sure are in attendance. Whether it's a key influencer in your group, leaders from local churches, a university professor, political

leaders, or successful entrepreneurs, how are you going to get them to the event? Who knows them or has a connection with them? Is a phone call or coffee appointment needed to extend an invitation? You may not necessarily need them to be onstage, but you want them there to hear about the issue and possibly leverage their resources (influence, notoriety, or money) toward the cause.

7. Utilize High-Quality Technology.

What technology will you need for the event, and is it already available at the venue? Do you need a sound system and microphones, video screen and projector, DVD or Blu-ray player, or special lighting? If the venue doesn't have it available, can you borrow it or will you need to rent it? Whether the venue has the equipment or not, who is going to be running it?

Someone the venue provides (and you pay), a volunteer from your team, or a professional company? In our present culture, we are accustomed to experiencing high-quality sound, video, and lighting at any event we attend - whether a concert, sporting event, or even most church services. Don't allow poor technology or unprofessional operation to become a distraction for your attendees.

8. Prepare and Post Clear Signage.

If people haven't been to the venue before, how will you help them recognize the location and ultimately your main entrance? Do you need a banner near the street? How about an a-frame sign near the entrance? Once inside the venue, is there signage that points them toward your meeting space? What about directions to the restroom? Printing a nicely designed sign with an arrow on 8.5x11 laminated paper is inexpensive and quick, but it will help people feel at ease. You don't want to make people ask for directions to something. Most people would rather see a sign and head that way on their own.

9. Recruit and Train Greeters and Ushers.

In order to make people feel welcome at your event - whether it's held at a private residence or a university auditorium, you'll want to have both greeters and ushers to create a connecting environment. Greeters are warm-hearted extroverts who are stationed outside the entrance to the venue, and the number needed is directly proportionate to the number of attendees who will be joining you. Instruct the greeters on how you want people to be greeted.

How to Host an EVENT

"Hello, welcome to _____."

Do you want them to wear a nametag? Are you providing it? Do you want them to actively shake hands with the people they are greeting (or not)? Have you reminded them to smile? Does the greeter need to know any pertinent information - especially where the restrooms are located?

While greeters are welcoming people to the venue, ushers (or hosts) are inside the room connecting with people, answering questions, and making people feel welcome. These are the volunteers who are most comfortable connecting with people they *don't* know. While many of the questions about greeters also apply to ushers, what are primary tasks of an usher? Passing out a program? Helping people find a seat? Ensuring that emergency exits aren't blocked? Assuming that volunteers who have been tasked with greeting and ushering know what you want them to do is a big mistake. They need to know the vision of the event, the desired outcomes, and how their role is critical to the success of the guest's experience.

10. Provide Refreshments (and Food).
At a minimum, you'll want to have water available to guests, but can you add coffee as well? Do you have volunteers who can prepare it? Or, do you want to purchase it from a local coffee shop and borrow their large containers for free?

I would like to caution you on the "potluck" approach to refreshments or food for a quality event like you'll be hosting. My guess is that you're not hosting a down-home church event, so don't treat it like one. Presentation can be just as important as the food or beverage itself. Consider fabric table cloths (versus plastic), a multi-leveled presentation (versus everything tossed out on a table), and nicely arranged napkins and plates.

When and where will the refreshments be available? Before the event to create a connection time prior to starting? Or, just coffee and water to keep people alert? Maybe the refreshments are served after the event to keep people around to talk about what they experienced? Or, maybe dessert is actually served during the event so that people can discuss the issue around their tables?

Who will be serving the refreshments? Adult volunteers, teens, or a professional catering service? What do you want them to wear? How do you want them to serve the refreshments? They won't know unless you instruct them. Remember, every detail adds up to create your desired outcome.

11. Ensure Proper Event Lighting.

Although it may be tempting to leave the lighting up to the tech guy in the sound booth, remember how powerful an effect lighting can have on someone's experience. Is the entrance and foyer well lit so that someone knows where to enter? If you're using a venue you're not familiar with, have you asked the appropriate person how to adjust the lights? Or, are the lights on a timer that needs to be adjusted? You don't want to be standing outside of your venue trying to call a custodian to come over and turn on the entrance lights. Then, once the attendee is inside the venue, what will the lighting be like? Will it change over the course of an evening? Is there enough lighting for people with poor vision to navigate through the room? Are there any obstacles that need to be moved or marked with brightly covered tape?

Years ago when I was a pastor, our church created an unusual stage for an Easter Sunday service, and a rather large woman tripped over the edge of stage because she couldn't see it. There wasn't enough room between the front row of chairs and this darkly-lit angled stage, and she fell and badly broke her elbow. After that accident, you better believe that lighting is important to me, and it should be to you as well.

12. Create an Attractive Look and Feel.

Every venue has an ambiance. The question is...does the venue's look and feel help or hurt your desired outcomes? Either way, how can you use physical props to create an attractive environment for your attendees? If you plan to move anything, take photos on your phone so that you can put the items back where they were. Then, rearrange chairs, shove the dusty silk flowers in a closet, and draw attention to what works for you.

The three most important places to be aware of the look and feel are the entrance, the gathering place where refreshments are served, and the area where people will be looking the most during the presentation (usually the stage). If you don't have an eye for interior design, ask someone for help. It's amazing how a venue can be transformed when you remove the clutter, cover things up with black fabric, bring in a few pieces of furniture, and display prominent signage or visuals that focus people on the cause.

13. **Remember the Power of Music.**
Almost everywhere you go, there is music playing in the background. When you walk in to almost any retail store, they are creating an atmosphere by playing some sort of music in the background, and you'll notice that it fits perfectly with the "vibe" of the store. What type of vibe do you want to create when people walk in? How can you utilize background music at volume that is not distracting? Do you want people to feel rested, joyful, high energy, or even dissonant? Create a playlist on your phone to play while people are arriving, during the event, or after it concludes to set the mood you want your attendees to experience.

14. **Design a Compelling Handout.**
If you're hosting an event about trafficking, my guess is you'll want to put something in the hands of each attendee - either as they walk in or during the experience. A physical program can be helpful if you want to them to know the flow of the event as well as the names, titles, and organizations of those who will be presenting. Yet, a program also somewhat limits your ability to change things up on the fly.

Whether you have a program or a handout of some sort, be sure that it matches the branding of the event. From the invitation to the social media presentation to the event handout, everything should match and provide a consistent message.

Ultimately, the primary message the program and/or handout should present is your "call to action." How do you want people to respond? Are you asking them to sign up for something or volunteer in some way? Are you inviting them to share their contact information with you via a perforated tear-off? Or, are you asking them to give via an envelope, text to give phone number, or special website URL? Make sure your handout provides a clear overview, a compelling reason, and an immediate next step to take action.

15. Staff an Information Table.
Beyond a handout, you may find it helpful to have an information table where people can go before or after the event to ask questions, turn in their envelope/tear off sheet, or write down their name on a sign-up form.

Make sure this table is staffed by people who represent your event or organization in the best way possible. They should be well-informed about the mission of the event, how to take action, and of course... where the bathroom is. The Information Table can have extra handouts, business cards of the presenters, and anything else that will help a person get involved.

16. Recruit and Prepare a Compelling Host.
Whether it's you or someone you recruit, the host is the face of the event, and he or she must align with your desired outcomes. They are the glue that holds the event together, and you definitely want the right kind of glue. If he's too funny, it can come off as insensitive. If she's too stiff, the event can feel stale and stuffy. If he doesn't know the subject well, the event can be awkward. You want someone who is sincere, has a heart for the issue, feels comfortable in front of people, and is willing to take direction.

Don't say "yes" to someone before you've seen them in action (at least on video). You want to see how they handle a room before giving over the reigns to the event you've strategically planned. If the host hasn't been part of the planning process, you'll need to walk them through the program from beginning to end - not just telling them what comes next, but telling them what's important about each aspect of the flow.

17. Type Up the Flow of the Event.
Even if it's an event for 10 people, I highly suggest you type up a flow of the event so you know what's going on from beginning to end. This allows you to think through everything from the music playing as guests walk in to the change in lights to the transition from one person to another. In order to stay on schedule, consider putting times next to each segment so that you know when that portion of the event is supposed to begin and end. Make copies and hand them out to your greeters, ushers, tech team, host, and all presenters.

18. Welcome Everyone to the Event.

At the beginning of your program, have the host introduce him or herself and welcome everyone to the experience. Let people know why you've gathered them together. It may seem obvious, but you're focusing everyone's attention on the reason for the event. In this moment, you have the opportunity to let them in on your desired outcome.

For example: "Tonight, we have gathered to learn about a tragedy taking place in our nation - sex trafficking. Not only will be watch a compelling documentary that will educate you on the nature of the issue, but I want you to be thinking about how you could host a screening of the film at your university, church, or local community center."

By telling them upfront what you're going to ultimately call them to at the end of the event, you're giving them a chance to process the experience in light of your upcoming "ask". They're already thinking about how they can get involved or take action. If you don't give them enough of a hint upfront about what you're calling them to (financial donation, volunteer, etc.), then they may feel less prepared or ready to say "yes" to your request.

19. Make Smooth Transitions.

Whenever there's going to be a transition from one thing to another (such as from person to person or from person to video to person), take time to think about and discuss those transitions with whoever is going to be involved. Awkward transitions and unnecessary pauses can create anxiety for those in attendance, and that won't help you reach your desired outcome.

You want people to know you are prepared and ready to share a compelling experience with them. In order to make smooth transitions, you'll want to think about where presenters are sitting, whether the mic is on or off, a clear phrase or sentence to provide a nice segue, and how lighting needs to change.

20. Keep People Engaged Throughout.

As you're thinking about the flow of the event, remember that the brain can't take in more than the butt can handle. After one to one and a half hours, people start feeling restless if they're seated. How are you going to keep them engaged in the event? Standing up and meeting someone new? Breaking into discussion groups? Walking around the stations in the room? Transitioning from an educational talk to a survivor story? What's it going to take?

If your event is not a seated presentation and it's more of a stand and mingle party, then how are you going to keep people engaged? Will there be live music, food to nibble on, seating vignettes to gather around, or a mixer game to help people connect? There's nothing worse than showing up to this type of event when you don't know anyone and you're somewhat of an introvert? Ask me how I know.

Just a few weeks ago, I was invited to an anti-trafficking event at a local hotel. The event was situated around a beautiful pool, but guests of the hotel were still swimming - even kids splashing around. The food stations were so dim that I had to pull out my iPhone flashlight to see what I was selecting. (Thankfully, the food was delicious.) The few attendees were scattered around the large courtyard, and it felt intrusive to join others in a cabana. My wife and I didn't know a soul, and no one was making an effort to connect people. Guess what? We left. I'm sure they have a great cause, but the event was incredibly awkward and prevented me from wanting to engage. How are you going to keep people engaged? That's the key.

21. Make a Clear Call to Action.

At some point during your event (usually toward the end), how are you going to call people to action? This is the compelling "ask" that will help you reach your desired outcome. Is this call to action being made by you, the host, or a guest speaker? Are you using images on the screen, the handout, or an envelope to help you in the process? Will you be asking them to make a decision on the spot, or are you giving them time to think about it?

22. Follow Up to Motivate Action.

Don't assume that someone will make a decision without a nudge from you or your team. Will you send personal emails to thank him or her for attending and a reminder about how they can take their next step? Do you want to send them a physical letter or postcard in the mail? Or, would it be most effective to give them a phone call to connect and ask them to take action in some way?

How to Host an EVENT

Two Friends Use Concerts to Combat Slavery

Five years ago, Grace Theisen came across an article on the Internet exposing the problem of sex trafficking in Michigan. After finishing her freshman year of college, she went home for the Summer and talked to her best friend, Lauren Lancaster, who serendipitously had learned about trafficking during the same semester. They quickly agreed that they wanted to use music to fight the injustice.

"Let's do a benefit concert!" Lauren exclaimed. So, they did. That first concert was in a tiny little barn in their hometown, and they ended up raising $4,000 for a safe house in Toledo, Ohio. Next Summer, they decided to do one more concert, and they raised double the amount - $8,000 for that same safe house.

Grace shared, "We were shocked by how many people didn't know this happened in the U.S. We also quickly realized that sex trafficking looks so different in every city and we would never be the experts. So we decided to use these events as a way to lift up those organizations who are already doing incredible work on the front lines."

Songs Against Slavery (www.songsagainstslavery.com) was born, and since 2011, they have organized 12 benefit concerts and raised over $30,000 for nonprofits in the U.S.

"Lauren and I could so easily talk about sex trafficking, but no one would come to the events because it is such a heavy topic. Pairing it with music gives such a hope and a light to this dark situation and allows us to be able to spread awareness in such a unique way. It also gives musicians a platform to use their voice from the stage and empowers them to join the fight."

Whether you're hosting a documentary screening, a guest speaker, or a volunteer training event, the first four questions we asked will guide you through your planning process. You have the opportunity to create an environment for people to be educated by trafficking and to be motivated to take action in a specific way. The degree to which you strategically plan, market, and host the event will largely determine whether you're able to reach your desired outcome.

Chapter Five

HOW TO RAISE MONEY THROUGH A CAMPAIGN

While I'm a big believer in the power of creativity, hard work, volunteers, and even personal favors, *money* is ultimately needed if we're going to put a stop to human trafficking in our world. It takes money to start projects, host events, launch campaigns, and found organizations. I wish finances were not required, but it's just a reality of the world we live in.

Frankly, raising money is one of the most challenging things I have had to do in life. Over the years, I have raised hundreds of thousands of dollars for both non-profits and business ventures, and in the last couple of years, I raised $30,000 to fund my first documentary and $85,000 to fund the recent production of IN PLAIN SIGHT.

You've got to know that I don't think I'm incredibly gifted at raising money nor do I have a list of wealthy benefactors. Instead, I attribute any level of success to two major things...

1. I only ask people for money to support something I'm deeply passionate about.

2. I have a deep belief that God will supply all the resources I need in order to accomplish the good works that have been prepared in advance for me to do.

Key Questions in Planning a Campaign

Once again, questions are the key to everything when you're starting your "something." These questions will refine your thinking and help you create a presentation that will equip you to raise the monies needed for your efforts.

- **Why are you raising money?**
    This may seem obvious, but the more clear the answer - the more money you have the potential of raising. If your reasons sound like "just helping out" or "trying to do good", the communication of your campaign will come off as nebulous at best and shady at worst. You want to be as specific as possible about how much you're raising and how it will be making a positive impact.

    Example #1: "We're raising at least $5,000 to help people know about sex trafficking in our city."

    Example #2: "[Name of group] is raising $5,000 to create and launch a strategic communications plan to educate churches within our city about the issue of sex trafficking and motivate them toward practical action steps."

    or

    Example #1: "We're trying to raise around $20,000 to help [name of aftercare home], because they do such great work for the women."

    Example #2: "[Name of group] is raising $20,000 to fix the leaking roof of the [name of aftercare home], who has served over 50 survivors of sex trafficking in the last year."

    Which campaigns would you rather give to? I'd definitely give to the second one, because there is specificity.

    I have learned to ask myself, "Do you have a campaign that shows potential givers that your efforts are truly worth giving to?" If not, I don't even ask.

- **Why do you need a certain amount of money?**
    Not only do people want to know why you're raising money, but they want to know what you're doing with it. If your answer is, "Because

How to Raise Money Through a CAMPAIGN

we think $5,000 should cover it", then you're in trouble. Big-hearted friends and family will probably still give, but not someone who is analytical or has much of a business background.

Before deciding on an amount you want to raise, you first need to determine how much your desired end result is going to cost. If you're raising money to fund a one-time project, a line-by-line budget with anticipated costs would be wise to have. Number one, you'll know what the project actually costs to complete, and number two, you'll be equipped to answer detailed questions when someone asks.

If you're raising money for another organization, most non-profits do not prefer what's called "designated giving" - a financial donation made directly for a certain purpose. It can be a bookkeeping challenge, and the money can *only* be utilized for that specific purpose.

Therefore, many fundraisers for other organizations will be focused on supporting their operating budget (general fund) to simply carry out the daily work they are committed to. If this is your focus, you are an incredible gift to that organization, because they definitely feel the weight of constantly raising money for their operation.

In the case of raising money for an organization's operating budget, you'll want to do two things. Number one, clearly articulate how the organization is making a tangible difference, and number two, quantify how the money will help the organization. For instance, "I am raising $1,000, which is the equivalent of two month's grocery expenses for [name of aftercare home], a residential program in our city that provides restorative care to survivors of sex trafficking." By helping people see how their dollars can tangibly help the organization, individuals will be more prone to give.

- **Who are your potential givers, and what motivates them?**
"Everyone" is not a clear enough answer. Of course, you want everyone to give, but some people are more likely to contribute than others. Friends and family will want to support you, but not all of them will. Go ahead and put their names down, but don't be surprised when one of them just "doesn't get it."

It can be disappointing when those close to us don't jump on board with something that's near and dear to our hearts, but keep moving.

When they see your commitment and passion, my guess is they'll want to join in at some point along the way.

Who else will you be targeting? In the coming pages, we'll be developing a strategy that includes emailing, calling, and setting up meetings in order to share the vision of what you're doing. Start thinking about who believes in you no matter what you're doing, who is generous in general, and who is interested in human trafficking in particular.

Whether they want the "backer reward" on a crowdfunding website or just the feeling of doing good, everyone gives money in order to get something in return. How are you going to motivate these people to give? Some will want to participate because they love and admire you, but others will need something else. For those who operate a bit more with their emotions, you'll want to ensure you provide them with that experience - not in a manipulative sort of way, but through the power of transformational stories you share with them. For those who are more analytical, additional facts and figures may be the driving factor behind his or her motivation.

- **What's your personal story?**
People want to hear about *your* experience. Why are you investing your own resources in this project? Did you see a news story that rocked your world? Did you meet someone who impacted your life? In other words, why does this matter to you?

    There are two reasons why your story is critical. Number one, people will be motivated by your story. In fact, this may be the most motivating factor in their giving. Your story will touch them. Number two, when things get challenging during the fundraising process, you can use your own story (your "why") to motivate yourself to keep moving forward.

Never Too Young to Help
After learning that the average age for girls trafficked into prostitution in the United States 12-14 years old, Emma Smiley realized that could be her. As a 12 year old living in Virginia, she was compelled to join the fight against human trafficking and immediately started brainstorming ideas about what she could do to raise money for the cause. "Scrubbies", a handmade dishwashing tool, was the answer!

How to Raise Money Through a CAMPAIGN

When word got out about her mission, churches from around the area started inviting her to come speak on the topic...and sell her Scrubbies. In fact, in her first year of fundraising, she raised over $2000 and has also hosted a community yard sale and a dinner and silent auction. She's now 15 years old, and she's already raised and donated more than $10,000 to help fight human trafficking.

Emma's passion is propelling her forward: "I am not done. I am convinced that every voice matters. The more people that know about it, the more people that have passion to do something, the more girls are saved and are rescued from this awful situation. My next event is going to be a global symposium that will be presented to my school to get my fellow classmates aware of this awful crime that affects millions of people everyday."

Ensuring Your Campaign's Success
Whether you're raising $500 by selling handmade items to benefit an existing aftercare home or $100,000 to fund a research project in your community, you will increase your potential for success by walking through the following steps. The more money you're seeking to raise - the more diligent you'll need to be each step of the way.

   1. Clearly State Your Desired Outcome.
   By answering the four foundational questions we just walked through, you should be able to state your desired outcome. It includes the amount of money you want to raise, what organization or group will be using the money, and how the money will make a positive impact. If you can't clearly state your desired outcome in one sentence, you're not clear about it yet. If you're not clear, no one else will be either. Get clear.

   2. Ensure a High Level of Trust.
   With every decision, ask yourself, "Should someone (and will someone) trust me with their donation?" Are you being clear about how the money is being raised, who it will be given to, and in what ways it will be utilized? If you're selling an item, are you clear about what percentage of the proceeds is going to the cause? Be clear, do what you say, and people will trust you.

   3. Make a Long List of Potential Givers.
   Pull out a piece of paper or open up a Word doc and start writing. I would encourage you to create four categories...

- Inner circle - close friends and family.
- Frequent contacts - people you have contact with regularly.
- Infrequent contacts - people you connect with 1x a month or so.
- Outer circle - people you know, but don't connect with often.

If you're selling an item to raise money, the same list applies to your efforts. Either way, you'll need a list of those who will want to support you in raising funds for a worthy cause.

4. Determine How You'll Raise the Money.
Perhaps, you want to run a race, host a dinner, paddle across a lake, organize a documentary screening, or start a crowdfunding fundraiser. Have you thought how much your methodology helps or hinders your contacts' interest in giving? If most of the people you're reaching out to are over 65 years old, crowdfunding via an online platform may not be the most successful method. Maybe hosting a dinner or dessert would work better. Or, if most of your contacts are young people on a limited income, a $100 per plate fundraising dinner could be a disaster. These two examples may be the extremes, but consider how you're raising money limits the amount you have the potential to raise.

The more a potential giver has an affinity with the methodology - the more likely they will be to give.

Keep in mind that using more than one methodology at a time may be confusing to your potential givers - unless you're a larger organization. If you have a big goal, one fundraiser may not provide you with all the funds, but I would encourage you to space them out a bit to avoid overwhelming people. In fact, you may find that the same people will give to both campaigns if they're separated by a few months.

In addition, be sure to give people as many ways to give as possible - cash, check, credit card, and PayPal. By having people make out checks directly to the non-profit or by donating online through the organization's website, you will increase trust and eliminate any hint of impropriety.

Unless you've been living under a rock, you're aware of crowdfunding websites like Kickstarter and Indiegogo. While an entire treatise could be written on this type of fundraising, my only caution is that you must take into account the cost of the "backer reward" and the cost of shipping the item(s) to the backer. This has killed many fundraisers in the past, and you don't want to find yourself in a position of not having enough money to actually send out the rewards you promised. I've launched several successful crowdfunding projects, and Tim Ferriss' overview has been the most helpful resource to me. Check it out at www.bit.ly/crowdfundingideas.

5. Carefully Choose the Date(s) to Hold the Campaign.
There are certain times of the year (and even times of the month) that are better for fundraising than others. If you're hosting a fundraiser that centers around a live event where you'll want donors to attend, avoid times of the year when people are out of town (summer vacations, holidays, and the like). If it's a multi-week campaign, are you taking into account any cultural conflicts at the beginning or end of the fundraiser? If you're launching a campaign in a community where finances are tight, are you aware of their pay days (i.e. 1st of the month)? Finally, are you aware of any other organizations who are making a major "ask" during the same timeframe as your campaign? Although you can definitely raise money during non-optimal times of the month or year, you may hinder the amount collected.

Another helpful tool may be a "bring your donation" event where people come to a physical event in order to hear more about the project or celebrate the fundraising process. This works well in churches where people are accustomed to gathering on a weekly basis already. Perhaps you plan a Friday or Saturday evening event where people bring their donations, listen to a compelling speaker, and hear an exciting announcement of the total amount raised.

6. Craft a 30 Second "Passion Pitch."
Based on your desired outcome (#1), write down a succinct "passion pitch" that could be given in 30 seconds to any one of your potential donors. After hearing your pitch, would someone be able to mirror back the amount of money you want to raise, what organization or group will be using the money, and how the money will make a positive impact (i.e., tangible outcome or measurable result)? To conclude your pitch, choose an appropriate question that invites the potential giver to take a next step.

"Would you like to attend the dessert?"
"Would you mind if I email you more information?"
"Will you consider giving online before (deadline)?"
"Are you open to helping me with this project?"

Practice sharing the pitch with a close friend, roommate, or family member. Ask them, "What isn't clear? Is there something that would make this more motivating?"

7. Determine if Public Recognition Will Be Given.

Recognition has been a strong fundraising motivator for as long as people have been raising money. There's something gratifying about seeing our name (or the name of a loved one) on a physical object or in print. This may or may not resonate with you and your project, but don't dismiss how motivating this can be to potential givers.

From posting their name on your website or social media account to engraving it on a brick to hanging a banner with their company's logo, you'd be surprised how excited people get about being recognized for their generosity.

As a sidenote, other givers may be just as motivated by anonymity. I've had donors swear me to secrecy, because they don't want the recognition nor do they want a bunch of other people contacting them for donations. Although it may be tempting to drop their name in conversation, you'll ultimately be hurting that relationship (and losing trust) if you don't honor their wishes.

8. Develop Motivating Communication Tools.

Beyond your passion pitch, you'll need some other communication tools to inform and motivate potential givers. This may be as simple as a photocopied flyer to as elaborate as a promotional video on your own website. Be clear about the need, the benefits, how to give, and the deadline. The opportunity to give must not be open-ended. People need to feel the urgency of an approaching deadline. Generally, people need 3-4 weeks to consider the opportunity to donate.

Be creative, positive, hopeful, and motivating. Although it's tempting to use fear tactics and negative imagery, I would encourage you to move people toward hope and restoration as much as possible. While fear may motivate people in the short-term, I think it ultimately pushes people away from wanting to be personally involved or take on a long-term role in ending human trafficking.

See Chapter Eight for a full list of communication tools that can be used to stand out from all the other "asks" being made of your potential donors.

9. Approach Your Inner Circle First.
Your inner circle is comprised of close family, friends, mentors, and even clients - people who love you and believe in you. They will be the most gracious when you stumble over your pitch, and they're also more likely to contribute than anyone else.

Depending on the type of relationship you have with each person, you'll want to approach him or her accordingly. When you're thinking about whether you email, text, call, or set up a coffee or lunch appointment, always think about it from the other person's perspective. What would be most helpful for them? Would a coffee appointment feel connecting or cornering? Is an email time-saving in their eyes or too impersonal? What would feel most comfortable for them (not just you)?

Whatever you choose, make it personal. This is not a business transaction. This is your passion, and that's what you're sharing. Sure, have your desired outcomes, strategy, and plans ready to articulate if and when appropriate, but this is someone who cares about you... and ultimately cares about what you're passionate about.

Don't be afraid to "make the ask." You aren't just giving them an updated on what you're doing with your life. You're actually inviting them to participate. You chose a question earlier when you were crafting your "passion pitch." Try it out. See if that question works for you in this setting.

Don't apologize in the process. You are inviting them to participate in amazing effort. In fact, you're doing them a favor by telling them about it. They get the privilege of participating, and they'll be able to say, "I helped make _____ happen." How cool is that?

Finally, you'll want to mention the deadline - not in a pushy way, but in a manner that helps them feel the urgency of their decision.

"I'm asking my friends and family to contribute by _____ so that I can go public with the campaign having already raised a portion of the goal. I would love for your contribution to be part of that initial announcement."

Notice what you're doing there. You're assuming they'll want to contribute. Why wouldn't they want to be part of your campaign? Even if they only give $10, $25, or $50, they'll get to participate in supporting you and this important cause. Don't forget to provide an easy way for them to give - either mailing in a check via an envelope you provide or via a website.

A few days prior to your "friends and family deadline", follow up with each person (via email or phone) and remind them that you'd like their contribution to be part of the initial announcement. Not everyone in your inner circle will meet this deadline, and that's okay. Many will join in at a later point in time when they see the momentum of your efforts.

If no contributions or only a small amount have been raised, you'll want to ask for some feedback. What's not motivating about your campaign or the way that you're communicating about the opportunity?

10. Go Public With the "Ask" and the Amount Already Raised.
Now that you have contributions in from some of your inner circle, you have the opportunity to go public with your ask. Although you may have developed a website, printed flyers, or crafted an email prior to this point, now is the time to spread the word and announce how much has already come in.

Consider a different level of communication for each of your lists of contacts - inner circle, frequent contacts, infrequent contacts, and outer circle. You may invite every Facebook friend to a Facebook event (utilized as a campaign announcement), but you might want to send individually addressed emails to your frequent and infrequent contacts. In fact, you may want to send a text or make a phone call to all your frequent contacts as well. Your approach will be based on your marketing plan which we address in a later chapter.

How to Raise Money Through a CAMPAIGN

As we've discussed, ensure that you're providing them with ways to give (cash, check, credit card, and/or PayPal) and a clear deadline that's not too far away or too soon. You want to have enough time to remind them about the opportunity a couple of times without being aggressive (too soon of a deadline) and without them forgetting about it (too far of a deadline).

11. Provide "Weekly Updates" Throughout the Campaign.
One of the ways to remind your contacts to give before the deadline is through regular updates - generally via email. These updates are weekly prompts that could include...

- How much money has been raised so far.
- Testimonials from people who have been impacted by the organization the money is going toward.
- Endorsements of the campaign by influential people.
- Interesting updates on progress.

With each update, you'll want to remind people why their contribution is so important, how they can make their contribution, and the deadline for giving toward the campaign. I would suggest including your phone number so that someone with questions is welcome to contact you. Whether someone actually does call you is beside the point. By making yourself available, you're letting people know that you're accessible to them and completely committed to the project.

12. Thank Donors Along the Way.
Rather than waiting until the very end of the campaign, take the opportunity to thank each donor individually immediately after they give. While an email is probably most appropriate, you may want to include a social media shout-out (with their first name) as well. While a few people may feel awkward, most people find it exciting and honoring to be mentioned in that way.

In the case of a larger donation, you may want to directly text or call the person to express your appreciation in a more personal way. Although it may sound odd to say that texting is personal, in many ways, it has replaced calling in our culture and may feel more comfortable.

If and when you see the donor in person, take a moment to genuinely thank them for their contribution, and let them know how much it means to you. Don't miss the opportunity to create a meaningful moment of appreciation and recognition.

13. Celebrate the Success of the Campaign.
After you've made your big communication push prior to the deadline, you'll want to celebrate the success and thank everyone who participated. Even if you didn't raise the full amount, focus on the positive things you'll be able to do with the money raised. Feel free to give people one last opportunity to give if they didn't have the chance or if they'd like to help reach the goal amount.

14. Follow Through on Any Recognition or Rewards Promised.
If you promised any recognition or rewards, be sure to follow through on what was articulated. Don't leave people asking, "When is my _____ going to arrive?" or "Why didn't I ever hear about my _____?" Although the campaign may have been a success, you'll lose the trust of others when you want to launch another campaign or project.

To ensure that you follow through on everything promised, keep a running list of every donor and what action step needs to be taken. When you've taken that action step (mentioned on social media, sent a thank you note, ordered the gift, etc.), make a notation that it has been completed.

15. Provide an Update on the Use of the Money.
A couple of weeks or a month after the campaign ends, provide an update to everyone (supporters and non-supporters alike) about how the money is being used. Be sure to connect the use of the donations with a tangible benefit.

"Because of the [amount raised], _____ was able to..."
"Thanks to your generosity, we were able to..."
"Without your contributions, we wouldn't have been able to..."

If you can include a story or quote from someone, the update will be even more powerful. Donors will be glad they participated, and they will have a great sense of satisfaction in joining your efforts.

How to Raise Money Through a CAMPAIGN

If you're going to raise money for any reason, you will serve yourself well to embrace an "abundance mentality" - the belief that there are more than enough resources available to do good things in our world. Instead of operating from a place of fear and scarcity, feel what it would be like to raise money from a place of abundance...

> **Scarcity:** I'll never have enough resources.
> **Abundance:** All the resources I need are available in the world.
>
> **Scarcity:** I am in competition with other groups.
> **Abundance:** There are many great causes in our world, but I am passionate about this one.
>
> **Scarcity:** I need to put other groups down to lift myself up.
> **Abundance:** I am passionate about this cause, and it is contagious.
>
> **Scarcity:** I don't trust people with my ideas.
> **Abundance:** By working together, we'll achieve even more.
>
> **Scarcity:** I want people to know it was my idea and hard work.
> **Abundance:** I am more concerned about the ultimate outcome than receiving the credit.
>
> **Scarcity:** This is a problem we can't overcome.
> **Abundance:** I am sure there is a solution.

With an abundance mentality, you're setting yourself up to develop a clear desired outcome, a powerful passion pitch, and a motivating call to action that people will want to say "yes" to.

Chapter Six

HOW TO START AN ORGANIZATION

Starting an organization is not difficult at all, but running and sustaining it is another matter. The road to ending trafficking is littered with well-meaning entrepreneurial types who want to do their part and end up starting a non-profit only to realize that funding their dreams and actually doing the work of the non-profit is a full-time, unpaid job…on top of the full-time job that actually pays his or her bills.

May I remind you of our discussion in Chapter One about "why" you want to start something? Before launching into non-profit waters, consider a few questions from someone who has done it…multiple times:

- Do you need to actually start an organization to do what you want to do?

- Is there another non-profit you could approach and offer to start a new program with them?

- Would it be possible to start a ministry within your church's existing organizational structure?

- What is it about starting a new organization that's necessary? The ability to raise funds and give people tax credit? The opportunity to lead an organization rather than having to report to someone else? The internal need to say you started your own organization?

- How will starting an organization truly empower you to do what you sense you are called to do?

If it seems like I'm trying to talk you out of starting an organization, you're right...I am. I want you to realize that it's more than just having a good idea and rallying a few people to give money.

If you're starting a non-profit, plan on a lengthy application for the IRS. You'll need to craft a clear mission, write explicit bylaws, recruit a board, and start raising money. People will start volunteering, and you'll be responsible for leading them through the ups and downs of the organization's journey. You'll need to update donors regularly, hire an accountant to oversee the books, and ensure that all monies are used for what they were intended for.

If you're absolutely confident in the need to start a new organization and committed to its long-term success, let's get started. I've outlined a list of action steps in a generally-recommended order, but you may find yourself tackling them in a different sequence.

PLEASE NOTE: *In no way is this chapter to be considered legal advice. I am not an attorney, accountant, or tax preparer, but I'm simply sharing the basic steps that are widely accessible for anyone wanting to start a non-profit. It is your responsibility to check with the IRS, your state and local governments, and any other licensing or permitting agencies in your state, county, or city to determine all necessary requirements.*

1. **Paint a Mental Picture of Your Preferable Future.**
   If you were to close your eyes and envision the future that you prefer, what would it look like? That's your vision. No matter what aspect of anti-trafficking you are passionate about, that's what will arise in your mind's eye. This isn't necessarily the methodology by which you'll make this vision come to fruition, but it's the result of your new organization's work. How would you conclude this statement?

   When I close my eyes, I envision the future of _____
   city, county, state, country

   having _____.

   What do you long to see? A transformed county legal system where victims are treated like victims and given the opportunity to experience restoration? Or, do you see a city full of teens aware of sex trafficking and motivated by educational and job opportunities (not the lies of a possible trafficker)? Or, maybe you envision numerous churches working together to operate in unison to combat labor trafficking in your area?

Remember, this isn't *how* your organization will carry out its work... it's what you envision as a *result* of it's work.

Now that you have the mental picture of your preferable future, write it down. Craft a sentence (or a few) that captures the essence of what you see. You'll want these words to capture the hearts and imaginations of all who read it. You'll want them to say, "Yes! I can see that, and I want to help make that come to fruition."

2. Recruit at Least Two People to Help You Get Started.
You might be able to start a project, event, or campaign alone, but I wouldn't recommend that for an organization. You need at least two other people to join with you in this tremendous adventure. One person needs to have an equal or similar passion for the issue and the way you want to go about tackling it. The second person should have a degree of experience in running a non-profit, and you'll want them to resonate with your vision although they may not be equally as passionate.

These two people will be your sounding board when you're wrestling with decisions, your fellow workers who are willing to carry part of the load, and your encouragers when you're feeling down or tired. Don't underestimate the importance of these two individuals. In an upcoming chapter, I'll address the opportunities and challenges of working with someone at this level of leadership.

3. Work Together to Craft A Motivating Mission Statement.
Now, as a team, you'll want to craft a mission statement that will articulate what your organization does. Although you're not doing it yet (whatever it is), you're stating this mission in the present tense.

Start by writing down everything that you want to do as an organization. Most likely, you'll come up with a long list of things that will be difficult to do in the beginning, but by listing it on paper, you'll see what everyone's desires are. Once it's down in writing, you'll want to ask yourselves, "Knowing that we can't do everything, what are the one or two things we want to focus our efforts on?"

Talk about it. Listen to each other. Kick it around. Wrestle through it.

You may start from either direction - crossing off things that are extraneous or circling the things that everyone is most drawn toward. If there isn't consensus about the focus of your new organization, let it rest for a day or even a week. Give people time to process it, and come back together again to keep working on it. This is the most important thing for any upstart, and you don't want to short-circuit the process.

As you're coming to a conclusion, take the time to craft a motivating mission statement in the present tense. Something powerful will happen as you state your mission as if you're already doing it. Not "our mission will be..." - it should be "Our mission is..." This is what you're doing as an organization, and it's starting right in that very moment.

4. Brainstorm and Select a Meaningful Name.
You may have been inspired by a word or phrase already, but consider the organization's name in light of your vision (mental picture of your preferable future) and the mission statement your team has developed.

If the name is too generic, it may not stand out from the crowd. If it's too nebulous, people may not have a clue about what it is. After making a list of possible names, you may want to run the options by a few people to ask them what they think. Ask them, "When you hear the name _____, what comes to mind? What do you think it is?"

Whether you end up going with a straightforward or super-creative name for your organization, I would suggest developing a tagline that flows from your mission statement. Although the name may be used to refer to the organization on a daily basis, the tagline can be a quick and clear statement that lets people immediately know what you're all about.

5. Hire Local Tax Attorney and/or Accountant.
Unless you want to do hours of research on your own or hire LegalZoom.com to get long-distance support, I would HIGHLY recommend getting a referral from a local non-profit or church to find a

qualified and experienced tax attorney and accountant. For a couple of thousand dollars, the tax attorney can guide you through the process of filing all appropriate forms - especially but not limited to IRS and state tax exemption.

You don't want to mess around and hope for the best. Hire a professional to ensure that it's done correctly the first time. Ultimately, this person will save you both time and money, and you'll have the peace of mind knowing that a trained professional is doing what they do on a daily basis.

6. Appoint Directors (Board Members) for Your Non-profit.

Most new nonprofits appoint their very first board members as part of the process of incorporating. When filing your "articles of incorporation", the state will ask for the names of the nonprofit's initial board of directors. If your state requires a minimum number of directors (three is common), you'll need to name at least that many in your articles. Although these individuals can be replaced at a later time, you might as well start off with people you truly want to work with. Their role will be outlined in the forthcoming "bylaws" which you will need to draft in order to file for federal tax exemption.

7. File Articles of Incorporation in Your State.

Filed with your Secretary of State, the organization's "articles of incorporation" establish the existence of your corporation in your state. They describe the basic characteristics of your corporation, and once approved, they legally create the corporation as a registered business entity within the state. Although you can receive assistance from your attorney or accountant, this is something that you probably can easily do on your own. Simply Google "filing articles of incorporation in [name of state]" and look past all the advertisements. Find your state's website ending in .gov, and follow the instructions. Although you may want to mail in your articles, you can often go to a local office to have them processed and approved on the spot. Get extra copies to keep filed away in a safe place.

8. Obtain an Employer Identification Number (EIN)

An Employer Identification Number or EIN (also known as Federal Employer Identification Number or FEIN) is the corporate equivalent to a Social Security number. Whether you ever plan to have employees or not, you'll need this number in order to open a bank account. Google "apply for an Employer Identification Number", and follow the instructions. You'll receive the number immediately online, and you won't have to wait for it to arrive via mail.

9. Open a Corporate / Business Bank Account.
Head on down to your local bank of choice and bring along your approved article of incorporation and your EIN. Ask how you can avoid any fees, deposit an initial amount of your choice, and order checks. Your debit card should arrive within a week, and you're ready to start spending the organization's money on organizational expenses.

Remember how you hired an accountant? Now, you'll want to provide him or her with requested information on a monthly basis - either statements, receipts, or both. Accounting will run you approximately $100-150 per month (which doesn't include filing other forms throughout the year).

10. Draft Bylaws of Your Organization.
Nonprofit bylaws are the rules and methods that your organization will follow to function legally and productively. Although they are required by the IRS when you apply for tax-exempt status, they are more of an internal document that includes a well-planned, clear structure taking the guess work out of how your organization is to operate.

This is the document that specifies the election of directors, your meeting process, the role of the employees, and many more details. Take your time when it comes to drafting your bylaws, because it's crucial to the future operation of your non-profit. Google "nonprofit bylaw examples" to see how others have approached this process.

11. Apply for IRS Tax Exemption (501c3).
To apply for tax-exempt status, you must complete IRS Form 1023, Application for Recognition of Exemption Under Section 501c3 of the Internal Revenue Code. Completing this form can be a daunting task because of the legal and tax technicalities you'll need to understand. As mentioned, hire a professional, and then plan to wait 3-12 months for the IRS to either send you a "determination letter" approving your status or requesting changes to your application.

12. Apply for State Tax Exemption.
Even if your organization has received a determination letter from the IRS denoting it as a federal tax-exempt non-profit, you ALSO have to do so within your state. If you don't, the state will come looking for corporate income tax on the money you have taken in from donors. Google "applying for tax-exempt status [name of state]", and follow the instructions.

13. Hold the First Meeting of the Board of Directors.
At the first meeting of the board of directors, you'll take care of formalities such as adopting the bylaws, electing officers, etc. After the meeting is completed, minutes of the meeting should be written and filed in the nonprofit's filing system set aside for official record keeping.

14. Take Immediate Action on All State and Federal Requests.
After applying at both the state and federal level, you'll start to receive mail from both entities. Don't let it sit on the counter and pile up. Open it, read it carefully, and ask your tax attorney and/or accountant any questions. If you need to prepare something, do it immediately. Don't wait until the deadline. Take care of it, and don't let anxiety or a lack of knowledge turn into procrastination. (Ask me why I know this.)

15. Organize and File All Documents Immediately Upon Receipt.
Yes, this is common sense, but you'd be surprised how quickly that envelope can disappear into a desk drawer. You don't want to be sitting across from your accountant with a blank stare when he or she asks you, "Did you receive something from _____?"

Get a few file folders, and label one "State" and the other "Federal". After you open the envelope, take the immediate action requested, and then file the papers accordingly. In addition, create a folder that says "Banking" and insert all banking records you want to keep to refer to at a later point.

By the way, you'll probably start to receive quite a bit of junk mail from companies who want to offer you all sorts of stuff - especially a merchant account to process credit cards. Throw it all away. If you need to accept credit cards, don't sign up for a multi-year contract through your bank or anyone else. The best deal I've been able to find is offered by Best Merchant Rates (www.bestmerchantrates.com), and they can help you receive payments online, in person, and even via one those fancy swipe-on-your-phone devices.

16. Keep a Record of All Communication with Agencies.
Whether a hand-written note on the appropriate file folder or in a Word doc, be sure to note when you communicated with any state and federal agencies (like the IRS). Don't assume that they'll get right back to you. Keep track of when you called, who you spoke with, what they said, and what action step you took. The same thing goes for mailing something. Record when you sent it and pay for postal tracking to ensure that the state or federal agency received the envelope.

17. Raise Money for Non-profit Activities.
Now, you're finally ready to start raising some money to actually do something as a non-profit. You may have already asked a donor (which could be yourself) to pay for attorney or filing fees, and all of those monies must run through the organization's bank account in order for the individual to receive a tax benefit.

Donations can be received while your application for state and federal tax-exemption is pending, and they may be treated as tax-deductible contributions retroactive to the date of your organization's formation. However, if your application is not approved, contributions can not be considered tax-deductible.

18. Start Actually Doing the Work of the Non-profit.
You can finally do what you set out to do as an organization. Recruit volunteers, raise up leaders, and get to work. Meanwhile, you'll continue raising money to fund projects, thinking about hiring your first staff, and partnering with other organizations to do great things.

For most non-profit founders, the work of starting an organization is completely volunteer, and many never receive a paycheck for the time and energy invested. It's a passion project, and it's fueled by your "why" and the mental picture of your preferable future. This is what it takes to start an organization. It's not to be taken lightly.

How to Start an ORGANIZATION

19. Ask Your Tax Attorney or Accountant Questions.
There will be moments along the way when you're dealing with finances, providing year-end tax receipts to donors, or receiving correspondence from the IRS that you won't know what to do. Don't try to wing it. Check in with your tax attorney or accountant and get solid wisdom. It's an investment of money to work with them, but ultimately they'll be saving you both time *and* money.

A Time and Season for Everything

After watching two compelling films (Call + Response and Slumdog Millionaire), Carrie Kuba began reading everything she could get her hands on about human trafficking. She started attending conferences, volunteering with various organizations, and hosting film screenings in her home.

"Over the course of about two years, it became very clear to me that there was nothing really available for moms, and by extension, families. And yet, from my vantage point, moms play the *most* pivotal role in combatting human trafficking! We are the ones who are raising the next generation of abolitionists, we are the ones most involved within our communities on a daily basis, we are often the ones in control of the budget and spending, thus the ones who can leverage our purchasing power, and we are the ones who have the ear of our spouses regarding donations."

In 2011, Carrie founded Someone's Child, an organization focused on engaging and empowering families to combat human trafficking. One of their primary tools was an Anti-Trafficking Toolkit, which was designed for families to keep in their homes and use as a resource to ignite discussion around the dinner table about modern day slavery, give practical ways the family could get involved, and provide additional resources. They also had a website and blog that provided more in-depth, current articles about human trafficking, monthly downloadables to keep their kits updated, and a calendar of national events.

"The irony of founding an organization for moms and families with the goal of helping bridge a family's extremely busy lifestyle with tangible ways to engage in anti-trafficking efforts is that that same target audience is often too busy to volunteer with an organization. I loved what I was doing, and I *still* believe strongly that it is needed, but I could not run an organization on my own. Not a healthy one, anyway. As more and more anti-trafficking organizations were coming out of the woodwork, it became abundantly clear to me that the movement didn't need just another organization - it needs more people involved. I realized that it was much better for me to let go of the organization and to therefore free myself up to be more involved in participating in the actual movement."

Although the organization Carrie founded is no longer in existence, she made a significant difference in the lives of families for over three years, and that's to be celebrated. What vision she had to create toolkits for families, and what courage she had to make the hard decision to conclude the organization's work.

Don't be afraid to say, "We're done"...or "I'm done." Figure out a way to celebrate what you've done, transfer the leadership to someone else, or even merge with another organization. None of that is failure. It's simply recognizing when the life of your organization has come to a point of transition. A strong leader won't let an organization limp along just because it "has to remain in existence." He or she will recognize the need for transition and graciously lead the way toward change.

All of that is to say...if you're going to start an organization, be ready to be in it for the long haul. This isn't a project or event or campaign. You're actually launching something that will become bigger than any one person. You're giving birth to something that has great meaning and purpose. Keep that mission at the forefront of everything you do.

Chapter Seven

RECRUIT AND MOTIVATE YOUR TEAM

Five years ago, Peggy Stapleton became aware of teenage girls being sold on the streets, just a few miles from her home in San Bernardino County, California. After meeting with the district attorney, police department, and other local government agencies, this mother of four recognized the need to start a faith-based group specifically focused on preventing and ending human trafficking in her county.

Through CADE (www.cadetogether.com), Peggy has recruited and formed an active task force of citizens, pastors, and key leaders in her area. Not only are they focused on raising awareness, but members of CADE have played a key role in helping to open a drop-in center and safe house called Rachel's House of Healing (www.forgottenchildreninc.org). With Peggy's growing network and a clear vision to open a "place of healing" for women, churches and individuals began to donate time and money to make this become a reality.

In mid-2012, a possible location became available, but it was in desperate need of repair. All the copper wire stripped and stolen, but an electrician donated five days of his time to re-wire the home. Members of CADE then came alongside to provide new flooring, new paint, plumbing, yard work, lighting, furniture for eleven rooms, and much-needed finances. CADE has also helped to staff the safe house, drop-in center, and street teams, as will as go to individual churches and bring awareness regarding human trafficking.

None of this would have been possible without Peggy's clear vision and her commitment to involving others in the process. Her passion and love for people is contagious, and others want to join her in the mission of ending trafficking in their county.

Noted author and leadership expert, John Maxwell says, "Teamwork makes the dream work," and that statement should be your driving mantra as you start your "something." Without a group of people who also have a mental picture of the preferable future and believe in the mission, your project, event, campaign, or organization aren't going to go very far.

While you may be starting with one or two other like-minded people, you're going to have to be intentional about recruiting and motivating other leaders and team members in order to carry out your mission. Over the last twenty years, I've learned my fair share of lessons from making *more* than my share of mistakes. Here are the most important principles that I've learned (often the hard way)...

Recruit a Lead Team of F.A.T. People
Although you may be doing almost everything yourself in the beginning, your eyes should be wide open looking for Faithful, Available, and Teachable people to serve on your Lead Team. This is a team of people who are committed to the "something" and are equipped to recruit team members for the cause. You want people who recognize they can't do everything on their own, and they are willing to seek out others to join the effort.

There's no need to officially call them your "Lead Team" until you see evidence of their leadership, but you can recruit them to help you get things started while observing their faithfulness, availability, and teachableness.

Here's a sample conversation...

> "I've noticed your passion for _____ and your ability to_____. I admire those qualities in you, and I would be interested in having you join our team. Would you be open to having a conversation about _____ (role description)?"

Recruit and Motivate Your Team

In a start-up situation, you probably don't want to hand them a finely-honed job description. You may want to discuss three to five bullet points that outline what you're looking for as a key team member or leader. The process of discussing the role and what you're looking for will help you and the other person refine what is needed.

Help Them Catch the Vision
More than anything, you want leaders and team members to catch the vision - the mental picture of a preferable future. Can they see what you see? They may not be able to see it as clearly, but can they catch a glimpse of the desired outcome? If so, they'll be motivated and driven to experience success.

In order to help them catch the vision, you may want to...

- Take them to a meaningful physical location.
- Give them a tour of a challenged area.
- Watch a documentary that educates and motivates.
- Have them read a compelling book on the subject.
- Expose them to another organization who has had success.
- Take them to a seminar, workshop, or conference.
- Share your heart and passion over and over and over again.
- Brainstorm a list of positive outcomes.
- Have them close their eyes and allow the mental picture to come to life in full color sights and sounds.

Because you're fully-focused on your "something", the vision lives inside of you powerfully, but you've got to realize that even your top leaders will forget it rather quickly. They'll get distracted by the details of the effort, and you'll need to constantly remind them why you're doing what you're doing. Keep the vision in front of your leaders and team members at all times.

Set Clear Expectations
If there's one thing I've learned in 20 years of leadership it's that you can't expect someone to do something you never clearly asked them to do. If you're particular about the task, be explicit or simply let it go. Otherwise, you'll be frustrated on the backside when the person returns without doing it like you would have desired.

Here's how I tend to couch any request...

1. **Set a clear goal.**
   Tell him or her what you want the end result to look like. If there are two or three things that you absolutely must have included, tell them as explicitly as possible.

2. **Set clear boundaries.**
   I envision this as the playing field on which the person is welcome to do whatever they like. The goal is downfield, but please don't do this (boundary) or that (boundary). Other than that, feel free to do whatever it takes to get the job done.

3. **Invite questions.**
   I always make myself available for questions in order to coach, clarify, or correct course. Call, text, or email if you have a question about anything, and I'll be happy to help.

In the end, there may still be unmet expectations, and that's an opportunity for a clarifying conversation.

"Oh, I thought you meant _____."
"Actually, I was envisioning _____."

Those conversations can be challenging, but they are an incredible opportunity to deepen relationships and clarify expectations for the next go around.

Help Them Set Their Own Goals
In the process of setting clear expectations, it is best to enroll your leaders and key team members by having them help set their own goals. "If our ultimate desire is to experience _____, then what are two or three goals we need to set in order to get there?"

Give them a few days to come up with the goals and associated deadlines, and then revisit the conversation. Have him or her share the goals, and you'll have the chance to listen to why each one is important to him or her. If you believe a goal is a bit off-track, you may say, "What about if...?" That's an opportunity to suggest an additional or different goal that will help them reach the ultimate conclusion you both desire.

Recruit and Motivate Your Team

Hold Regular Team Meetings
Whether you have one leader or a room full, take the time to hold regular team meetings that are meaningful. Don't just meet to meet, because people will feel like you're wasting their time. In every team meeting, I hold, I like to do three things...

1. **Celebrate success.**
   Take a few minutes at the beginning of the meeting to ask your team, "What do we want to celebrate since we last met?" Then, start by modeling the type of answer you want others to share.

   You may say, "I want to celebrate how Bob did such a great job nailing down the location for our upcoming event. I like how you researched numerous locations and helped us find a low-cost, high-quality option."

   By celebrating success, you're using positive reinforcement to encourage similar behavior by everyone on your team. It also creates a momentum-building atmosphere that's contagious.

2. **Learn from your challenges.**
   Not only do we want to celebrate, but we want to learn from our challenges and mistakes. Next question around the table is, "What do we want to learn from since we last met?"

   Once again, model an answer by being genuine in a learning you've experienced recently. Share what was a challenge for you and how you came to some sort of enlightenment in the process. By making learning from challenging situations the norm, you're giving people permission to make mistakes and grow as a leadership team. Constant learning is a sign of a healthy team.

3. **Plan for the future.**
   There's really not much a reason to meet unless you're going to take ground by talking about the future. If you're starting "something", that means you're wanting to make forward progress. You're seeking to accomplish something, and that's the focus of most of your discussion at your team meetings.

   Come prepared with a pre-planned agenda of items to discuss. Consider reading the list, confirming what time the meeting is to conclude, and ask if there are any other important agenda items to add to the list. Once you've quickly solidified the agenda, get down to business. Watch the clock, manage your time, and keep the discussion moving toward action steps. Always conclude the discussion by answering the question, "What needs to be done by what day by whom?"

Affirm Positive Character Qualities
As you engage in the work of your "something", look for opportunities to point our positive character qualities in the people you are working with. There's nothing more life-affirming than genuine words of affirmation. We live in a world of criticism, and I am probably one of the worst offenders. That's why I have to raise my antennae and focus my attention on the positive I see in other people. Not only does it make him or her feel good, but it reminds me to focus on that which I want to cultivate more of.

Appreciate Great Work
While affirmation focuses on character qualities, appreciation is all about performance. When someone does a good job, point it out in front of others and cheer them on. Look for ways to draw attention to a detail or uniqueness of what they accomplished, and let them know you are thankful for their efforts. If you want to motivate people you're working with, focus less on what needs to be better and more on what's going well. Appreciation *is* motivation.

Listen to the Ideas of Others
Yes, you're passionate about your "something", and you have a vision for the future, but you're also rallying experienced and thoughtful leaders to join you on the journey. Ask lots of questions, and listen to them. Some of the suggestions will be their own personal pet peeves, but others will be golden.

Start with, "What do you think about...?"

End with, "Thank you for sharing all those ideas. I'm going to think about what you've said and take that into account as we move forward."

Don't say that as a way to blow them off and move on. Genuinely listen and think about their perspective. I would go so far to say that each of your leaders and team members have been put in your life for a reason. Learn from them.

Recruit and Motivate Your Team

Take Responsibility for Personal Issues and Mistakes
If you haven't figured it out yet, we're all jacked up in one way or another. We have "personal issues" that stem from our families of origin, our unique personality, and the experiences we've walked through in life. These issues can cause us to respond in ways that are less than helpful in a leadership or team-based atmosphere.

If you're not already aware of what's going on beneath the surface of your mind and heart, you may find these two books helpful...

- *The 7 Habits of Highly Effective People: Powerful Lessons in Personal Change* (Steven Covey)
- *The Wounded Healer* (Henri Nouwen)

I have found that therapy with a licensed marriage family therapist (alone and with my wife) to be extremely powerful over the course of the last 20+ years. It's not a sign of weakness, but strength.

As you react in ways that are less than helpful, acknowledge the challenge, and seek to rectify any negative repercussions. When you make a mistake, admit it quickly, apologize for the error, and clean up the mess as soon as possible. By admitting weakness, you are modeling for your team that humility, forgiveness, and grace are needed for (and from) everyone.

Don't Put Up With Triangling
Unfortunately, there will be times when someone on your team chooses to *not* deal with a challenging situation directly with you. Instead, he or she may choose to go to another person on the team and vent, gossip, or slander. Processing their emotions and the issue itself in order to approach you is one thing, but causing dissension through triangling is another.

Make it clear to everyone on your team, "When you have a challenging situation or disagreement with another person, first of all, seek to understand. Second of all, have the conversation directly with that person - not with another person."

Help people understand that this is the normative way to deal with conflict on your team.

Share with your team, "If someone approaches you to complain, moan, groan, or gossip about someone else's behavior, strongly encourage them to speak with the person they have an issue with. Let them know that you are not a dumping ground for their problems."

You want to simultaneously encourage healthy communication and discourage any communication that's going to tear down your team or the success of your "something."

Maintain Your Momentum

There will come times when you or your team are tired, discouraged, or just feel a little "blah." It's good to acknowledge it, but it's your job as a leader to help the team regain and maintain momentum.

Here are three proven ways to get momentum going again...

1. **Revisit the "why" behind what you do.**
   You may be so caught up on the mundane aspects of doing what you're doing that you forget the very reasons why you started all this in the first place. Remember your "why."

2. **Remind your team of the vision.**
   Keep that mental picture of your preferable future out in front of you. Don't forget the ultimate result you're working toward. Close your eyes, see it, hear it, smell it, and remind yourself of your desired results.

3. **Re-tell stories of success or transformation.**
   Who or what has been impacted by your work already? Tell the stories even if they're familiar. Have someone whose life has been transformed come and share their story in person. This will remind you of your "why" and your vision simultaneously.

Raising Up a Team to Transform a County

After coming to faith just seven years ago, Marguerite Hawes became aware of trafficking in South East Asia by watching a television program, and she was filled with deep sorrow and grief. She tried to put aside her newfound awareness and the resulting emotions, but more experiences began to re-affirm her need to take action.

After meeting with leaders at her church, she hosted a conference on human trafficking to increase awareness and start connecting churches around this issue. In the process, San Joaquin County Justice Coalition

Recruit and Motivate Your Team

(www.sjc-jc.org) was launched with the purpose of engaging and mobilizing the Christian community to develop a comprehensive collaborative response to modern day slavery in San Joaquin County.

By rallying a team of people, Marguerite has been able to begin leading street teams in high risk areas to educate businesses and hotel employees while also looking for local runaways. Her team has also drafted an anti-trafficking/anti-slavery resolution that was sponsored by two city council members and passed in October 2014.

Marguerite shares the heart behind the effort, "The purpose of San Joaquin County Justice Coalition is to communicate to our community. When we go out looking for a missing child, we are communicating that there is no such thing as a throwaway child. When we go to hotels and other high risk establishments and educate the staff about trafficking, we are communicating that are eyes are open and that light is being shone into the dark places. When we speak with legislators and city officials, we are communicating that the least of these have an advocate."

There's no way Marguerite could do this without a team of people who are committed to ending human trafficking. She has helped them catch the vision and leverage their resources to impact the county in which they live.

If you implement these simple leadership principles as you start your "something", you'll be well on your way to recruiting and motivating a powerful team. Teamwork does make the dream work, but it can also be challenging. That's why it's not something for the faint at heart. Having made it to this point in the book, I would say that you're definitely committed to moving forward, and you're passionate about your "something".

Are you ready to get the word out?

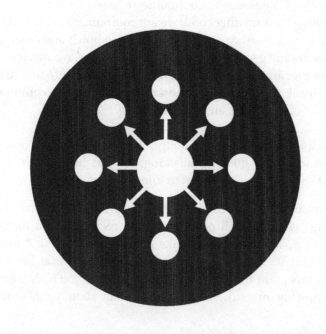

Chapter Eight
MARKET YOUR SOMETHING

Whether you're launching a project, hosting an event, raising money through a campaign, or starting an organization, you're going to need to use every means possible to market and spread the word about your "something." With a plethora of online tools now available, there's no excuse for low-quality communication tools. You can have a cohesive marketing effort, but it's going to take a little work.

You can work for months on your "something", but if no one knows about it, you're not going to experience the success you've envisioned.

Key Questions in Creating a Marketing Plan
When I consult businesses and non-profits on a marketing plan, there are several key questions that I ask them at the very beginning of our conversation. It may be fun to start talking about website domain names and social media right off the bat, but the answers to these simple questions will form the foundation for all future communications.

- **What is your mission? What are you trying to accomplish?**
  Yes, we've discussed this in every section, but you've got to be able to articulate it succinctly and clearly. When someone asks me, what is the purpose of IN PLAIN SIGHT, I say, "The IN PLAIN SIGHT documentary and accompanying resources are designed to educate America on the issue of sex trafficking and motivate them to take action in their community."

  When I first started developing the idea behind the documentary, I didn't have that sentence down quite yet. It took me a few months to refine my "passion pitch", but I was very intentional about the process. Even if you're simply hosting a one-time event, people want to know what your mission is. Figure it out and refine it until it flows out of your mind and heart with passion.

- **What is unique about what you're doing?**
Without uniqueness, you won't stand apart from the crowd. What is "remark-able" about your project, event, campaign, or organization? What is able-to-be-remarked about? While your mission is what helps people understand what you're doing, your uniqueness is what people will be talking about for weeks to come.

What's different about what you're doing than everyone else who has done something similar? It's not about putting them down, but it's about distinguishing your efforts. You're not doing this to pat yourself on the back or say "look how great we are." You're doing this uniquely so that people will actually hear your message and take notice in the midst of thousands of other messages being thrust upon people on a daily basis.

With IN PLAIN SIGHT, there are three things that I share with people to help the film stand out from the crowd. Number one, the focus of the documentary is the work of six female abolitionists who have leveraged their life to do something significant for survivors of sex trafficking. Yes, we educate people on the issue of sex trafficking, but our main focus isn't on victims. It's on these passionate abolitionists. Secondly, our approach is centered on *stories of hope and freedom*.

In fact, we made that the tagline for the film, because we wanted to distinguish ourselves from the depression that's often the result of watching other documentaries on trafficking. Finally, we created a film that wasn't sexualized or titillating in any way. It's real and raw in it's discussion, but we didn't feel the need to re-create scenes or make the viewer feel like they had just stepped out of an adult bookstore.

- **What is your story?**
People are going to ask you why you're doing this. Why are you starting this project or hosting this event? Why are you raising money for this organization? What has compelled you to take action?

Market Your Something

This may or may not appear in most of your communication materials, but it will fuel and inform them. You better believe people (especially friends and family) will want to know why you're investing so much time and effort in your "something." People are interested in you and your story. Be ready to share it.

Friendship and Fair Trade
Fueled by friendship and a mutual passion to end human trafficking around the globe, Fay Grant and Michelle Fergason started The Tote Project (www.thetoteproject.com), selling fair trade tote bags that are manufactured by survivors of sex trafficking in India and donating a percentage of their profits to safe houses and abolitionist organizations in the United States.

Fay explains, "Our business grew out of the necessity that people understand those who have been abused or trafficked are not weak or cowardly; they just don't have the help, love, knowledge or resources to use their strengths to overcome their circumstances. The Tote Project is our way to shine a light on human trafficking and show people that in spite of how overwhelming the statistics and circumstances are, we all have the ability to make an extra effort, no matter how small, to reach out and positively impact the lives of others."

After spending a year developing a business plan and the bag designs, they've had tremendous success in a short amount of time. Not only has The Tote Project been featured on Huffington Post and multiple fashion blogs, but Fay and Michelle were invited to SoulFest in New Hampshire last Summer where they led a workshop on "Fashion For Freedom" and got to share The Tote Project's mission with over 10,000 people on the main stage of the festival.

To take their line of bags to the next level, they launched a crowdfunding campaign on Indiegogo and employed several unique marketing strategies in the process. Not only did they offer a "Bob Goff package" including an autographed copy of *Love Does*, but they also gave away sixteen autographed totes to sixteen lucky winners from a pool of people who gave toward the campaign and actively shared about it on social media. The autographs were from well-known musical artists such as Moby, Switchfoot, the cast of Glee and many more, and guess where they got them? Yep...at SoulFest where they shared about the project last Summer.

Brilliant!

START SOMETHING TO END TRAFFICKING

Over the next few pages, I want to share my process of creating and launching a low-cost, high-impact communications plan. Marketing happens to be one of my passions, but I want to show you how you (and your team) can utilize all of these tools to spread the word about the gret things you are doing.

Naming Your "Something"

No matter what you're starting (a project, event, campaign, or organization), it needs a memorable name. You want people to be able to refer to it and not say "that thing you're doing."

There are two approaches I take when I name something - either naming it so that people know what it is right from the start or naming it something creative so it evokes a need for further conversation. The first has the possibility of coming off as ordinary or boring, and the second has the potential of being downright confusing.

With the mission and uniqueness of the "something" in mind, I make a long list of possible names. No name is a bad name. I just type and type and type until I can't think of anything else. I rearrange words. I make up words, and I look up words in a thesaurus.

Once I have a long list of names, I ask myself these questions:

1. Which name inspires me?

2. Is there anything associated with the name that is confusing or negative?

> For example, there is a restaurant near my house called "Rance's Pizza Place", and I'll never go there because it sounds like "rancid pizza" to me. It might seem silly, but I wonder who else is thinking that.

3. Is the name too similar to an existing well-known entity?

4. If people won't know what it is immediately, is there a tagline that will work well with it?

After I've narrowed down the list to two or three options, I usually email them to a small group of people whose opinion I value. I'll write something like...

Market Your Something

Hi _____,

I'm in the process of naming a _____ that I'm starting, and I value your opinion. Out of the three names below, which one is the most engaging to you? Is there anything confusing or troublesome about any of these names? Any other suggestions?

Name 1
Name 2
Name 3

Thanks,
David

After receiving their response email, I'll often call them back and ask for further feedback or ideas. Meanwhile, I've been trying the names over and over in my mind, I'll same the outline to see how they sound. How does it sound to say...?

"I'm excited about _____." (project)
"Are you going to _____?" (event)
"How much money have you raised with _____?" (campaign)
"When is the next _____ meeting?" (organization)

Once you've named your "something", you'll start to feel it take on a life of its own. There's something powerful about the name, and it will create initial momentum for you and your team.

Logo, Colors, and Fonts

Depending on your budget, there are five ways to go about creating a look and feel for your "something", but it all starts with the graphical treatment of the name you just decided upon.

1. Professional Graphic Designer - $500-1000

To hire a graphic designer in your area to create a series of three possible logos based on your conversation with him or her, you'll need to be ready to spend $500-1000. After you choose one of the logos you like, they'll generally provide you with up to three revisions to tweak it to your liking.

2. Crowdsourced Designer - $299

If you have a few hundred dollars to invest, having a logo designed by graphic designers from around the world on 99designs.com is well worth your money. You'll receive 30+ possible designs from numerous designers, and you can ask for modifications from the designers along the way in order to create just what you envision. I've used this service multiple times, and the experience (and final logo) always exceeds my expectations.

3. Overseas Option - $5-100

If you're willing to wade through possible candidates, you can find someone to create an amateurish logo for as low as $5 on Fiverr.com or upwards of $100 on Elance.com or oDesk.com. All three of these services connect you with world-wide contractors who will do all sorts of work for you - including graphic design. It can be a lot of work to sort through the resumes, communicate with someone whose English may be rough, and deal with global time zones. Proceed with caution.

4. A Friend - ?

If you have a friend who has graphic design skills, you may be able to barter services, ask for a favor, or show up with a pizza to get them to help. I have found two main downsides of working with friends. Number one, you're probably going to be last on their list of priorities - far behind their paying clients. Number two, asking for revisions can get touchy if they're donating their services. Yes, the logo might be free, but there could be a high cost.

5. Yourself - $0

If you have Adobe Photoshop or Illustrator, you've probably messed around enough to pull off something on your own. If not, Google "free logos" and get creative. In a worst case scenario, choose an interesting font (not Papyrus or Curlz), and use that font for your logo.

In the process of creating a logo, you'll want to select two main colors and another primary font. These two colors (plus black or dark gray) will function as your color palette for the rest of your marketing, and the font used in your logo can often be used for headlines or main points. A second font should be something you use for the majority of the text copy in your promotional materials - something easily readable, such as Helvetica, Myriad Pro, or even Arial. If you feel like those fonts are too heavily used for your taste, choose something else, but I would encourage you to think about readability with everything you put out into the world.

Now that you have a logo, colors, and fonts, you're ready to create more marketing resources.

Business Cards
Although traditional business cards are still quite popular in the business world, I like to opt for a combination business/promo card when it comes to non-profit or cause marketing. You can put your name and contact information on one side and promo information about your project, event, campaign, or organization on the back including tagline, bullet points, website, or action step.

The options for business card design are essentially the same as your logo, but I'd like to throw in three other companies that might be a good way for you to go...

1. **NextDayFlyers.com**
   I've been using this company for years to print almost all my business cards and promotional materials. In my opinion, they have the best combination of quality, price, and service. If you have the ability to design your own business card in Photoshop or Illustrator, I would use them to print the cards. Although they have an online interface to design a business card online, I wouldn't say that is their strength.

2. **Vistaprint.com**
   Not only do they print anything and everything, but they have a handy interface to upload your logo (or not) and create a business card with one of their templates. Or, you can hire them to create a business card for you for as low as $49.

3. **Moo.com**
   For a non-traditional option, Moo.com offers professional and unique designs that you can use by simply entering your own information. These are extremely high quality cards, but you're going to pay more for them.

When you're designing your business / promo card, be sure to consider cohesiveness of your marketing resources. Don't buy a super-cool business card from Moo.com and never use any of that look and feel anywhere else. Constantly be thinking, "How am I going to ensure that everything matches and looks similar?" If you hired a professional graphic designer, he or she would ensure that your logo, business cards, flyers, and website all match. Yet, if you can't afford that in the beginning, you'll need to ensure that yourself.

As a sidenote, business cards (especially from NextDayFlyers.com) are extremely inexpensive. If your business card is doubling as a promo card, order as many as you can afford. Don't skimp on the amount. 5,000 business cards may seem like a ton, but you can give them out liberally and leave them everywhere. (Just remember that your contact info will be out there for the world to see as well.)

Flyers, Brochures, and Posters
Frankly, you may not need other printed materials depending on the situation. For many of the things I work on, I don't even bother creating professionally printed materials. Most of my communication and marketing is happening online or via email, and printing flyers just leads to unnecessary expense and waste.

If you're in a situation where printed materials *are* needed, your best bet is obviously professional design. If you can't manage to acquire that through payment or bartering, you can create everything yourself. Although it's not the best option, Microsoft Word can be used to create a two-up flyer. In "page setup", you can change the document from portrait to landscape, and then you can add a second column. With two columns, you can create a front and back of a flyer quite easily.

You can save it on a thumb drive and take it down to your local office supply stores, and they'll happily help you photocopy it nicely. If you're not a professional designer, I would encourage you to stay away from a full-color design. Generally, it just looks bad, and black ink on a color paper will serve you much better.

Website - Your Online Hub
With the myriad of online tools available today, it's easier than ever to put up a website without hiring someone to assist you. There's absolutely nothing wrong with using a free or purchased template in order to launch a web-based home for your project, event, campaign, or organization. Here are three low-cost, no-cost options for you to consider...

Market Your Something

1. **Website Builders (paid)**
   There are numerous companies who have created "website builders" that allow you to build and customize a website for a monthly fee. For as little as $1 per month, you can create a simple, yet fully-functional website with your own domain name (www.yourname.com) by using GoDaddy.com or 1and1.com. Yes, it takes some time to think through your domain name, template, and content, but it's not hard at all.

2. **Website Builders (free)**
   In addition, there are numerous websites that will let you create a free website with a unique domain name, but it will have their company's name included. One such platform is called Wix.com, and they have beautiful templates to choose from. If you aren't willing to pay a monthly fee, they'll keep their name in the URL (yourname.wix.com), and they'll display advertisements on your page as well.

3. **Wordpress.com (free or paid)**
   As of August 2013, the Wordpress platform was used by more than 23.2% of the top 10 million websites. It is both powerful and flexible, and I use it for almost all my clients' websites. While you can go through the process of downloading the platform at www.wordpress.org, installing it on a server, and modifying it, you'll probably want to opt for the second, easier method. By using www.wordpress.com, you don't have to download anything, but you'll have access to the power of Wordpress and be able to use your own domain name as well (www.yourname.com).

No matter what platform you choose, you'll want to ensure that the platform is "responsive" - meaning the website layout changes if a person is browsing via desktop, tablet, or phone. Do NOT choose a template that is not a "responsive" theme. An increasing percentage of users will be engaging your website via tablet and phone, and you want your content to be displayed in the best possible way.

Now that you've chosen a web platform, it's time to develop the content for the website itself...

- **High Quality Photos**
  While most of the templates you'll be using have existing photos, you'll want to replace them with images that capture your unique

mission and message. Either, you'll use high-quality images that you or someone you know has taken, or you'll be using stock photography. If you opt for stock photos, do NOT take them from someone else's website. Companies who own those images (such as Getty Images) have the ability to track you down and send you an enormous bill. I've had multiple friends deal with this high-cost situation. Instead, I would suggest DollarPhotoClub.com for a low-cost, high-quality option. Yes, every image is literally one dollar.

- **Home page**
Clearly state your mission and uniqueness in words and pictures so that people immediately know what you're all about. Then, consider what action step you want them to take. Volunteer, register, donate, or get involved? Choose a "call to action" that is prominent on your home page and throughout the website.

- **About page**
This is often the second-most viewed page on a non-profit's website, because people want to know what organization or individuals are behind the effort. Share the story of why you're doing what you're doing and draw in the viewer.

- **"Something" page**
This is the page where you go into detail about whatever your "something" is. Name it whatever makes sense - Our Campaign, Our Cause, Our Mission, Our Purpose. Elaborate on your mission, your uniquenesses, and how people can specifically get involved.

- **News/Blog page**
This page will contain updates about what you're doing. Rather than a personal blog, it should take on the perspective of the project, event, campaign, or organization. It is an official communication that shares stories and updates. If you're wanting to create a greater level of interactivity, you may opt to turn the comments "on" for your blog posts. Yet, if you're not going to have someone oversee the occasional comment, encourage comments, or deal with spammy comments, I would suggest turning them "off."

- **Take Action or Contact page**
While you may want to opt for the standard Contact page where you put your phone, email, address, and/or contact form, some organi-

Market Your Something

zations are shifting to more of a "Take Action" page that outlines a next step (and includes contact info). Your goal is for people to take action - not to just contact you. Therefore, labeling it in that manner may be helpful.

- **Social Media Icons and Links**
  With your website as your online hub, your social media accounts are outlying points of daily/weekly communication. These are the places in which you form online connection and community, and you'll definitely want people to know where to connect with you by including your social media links on your website. Most all the templates you will be considering will have the ability to insert these important links with each social media icon (Facebook, Twitter, Instagram, YouTube, Vimeo, etc.).

Social Media Accounts
Social media will be one of the most powerful ways that you can spread the word about your project, event, campaign, or organization. Rather than go into detail about all the different social media platforms, I want to recommend two books that have been extremely helpful to me...

- *Platform: Get Noticed in a Noisy World* (Michael Hyatt)
- *Jab, Jab, Jab, Right Hook: How to Tell Your Story in a Noisy Social World* (Gary Vaynerchuck)

Notice the key word in the title of both books..."noisy." Everyone has something to say on social media, and the challenge is how to get your message heard and how to develop a community of people who truly care about what you're doing. These two books are your best bet if you're serious about doing something other than just adding to the noise.

Facebook Marketing
Because Facebook has now throttled the number of people who see our posts, they are forcing us to pay for access to our own followers. Even though that drives me nuts, it's still a great way to spread the word about your "something".

You may have noticed the "Boost Post" button, and that's definitely one way to get an important post noticed for a few dollars. I would suggest that you go to www.facebook.com/ads and check out how you can target people through Facebook advertising. I've found it to be incredibly helpful in gaining page "likes" and drawing attention to an upcoming event. You can drill down to a specific demographic and target people who "like" your page or even the pages of others.

Email Updates
Because social media has become so noisy and Facebook has throttled your followers' ability to see your posts, email continues to be the *best* way to directly communicate with people who are interested in your "something." Capture emails every chance you get. Whenever someone signs up or communicates with you about anything, get their email address and include a simple request to add them to your email update.

I would recommend signing up with Mailchimp.com or MadMimi.com to create a high-quality email newsletter. While MailChimp.com currently has a free option for up to a certain amount of emails, the low cost of either email platform is well worth the ease of connecting with your followers on a regular basis.

The bottom line is...keep your followers informed with something that is both new and engaging. Don't just send an email to send an email. Tell them something new, share an inspiring story, and always call them to take action. Don't ever send an email that doesn't have some sort of action step that you're moving people toward (volunteer, attend, sign up, register, donate, etc.)

Be thoughtful about how often you send the email so as not to agitate your followers. During a busy season, you may want to send an email once a week, but in non-busy times, perhaps it's every other month.

Finally, be aware that there are two main factors that determine how many people will open and read your email - the day/time in which it was sent and the subject line. If you click "send" on your email in the middle of the night when you've frantically completed it, the message is likely to be buried in the midst of all the other late evening emails. Yet, if you send it at 10am on Tuesday, Wednesday, or Thursday, it will have a higher likelihood of being opened in the midst of a non-frantic workday.

Now that the email has landed in your follower's inbox, the question is, "Will he or she view it as a spammy nuisance or something intriguing?" If your subject is simply the name of your organization followed by the word "update", don't expect too many opens. Instead, craft a subject line that teases the reader in the form of a question or statement - calling for them to click the email and discover the answer.

Personal Emails
When you're rallying people to support your project, event, campaign, or organization, personal emails can be a genuine way to spread the word and connect on an individual level. These have a more personal tone than your mass email updates, but clear, inspiring communication is just as necessary. Here's my formula for a connecting, informative, and motivating email...

>Hi _____,
>
>I hope you're having a great week [or some other personal point of connection that you have].
>
>I wanted to let you know about _____ [one-sentence overview].
>
>**Bold Headline**
>More information, dates, time, location, etc.
>
>To _____ [get involved, register, attend, donate], be sure to _____ [action step] by _____ [deadline].
>
>Thanks so much!
>David
>email@email.com
>xxx.xxx.xxxx (cell)

Notice that I connect with the person in the beginning, and then I give them a one-sentence overview about why I'm contacting them. I use a bold headline such as (Our Upcoming Event, How You Can Help, etc.) to quickly draw their eye down to the next line, and then I give them all necessary information.

I never embed a date, time, or location deep in a paragraph. It's just too easy to miss. Instead, I make it stand out with the date and time on it's own line and the location on another. Use spacing, bold, and underlining to help the information pop out for the reader's eye.

START SOMETHING TO END TRAFFICKING

Phone Calls

There's an old-fashioned method of communication called a telephone that I've found to be quite helpful when spreading the word about a project, event, campaign, or organization. I know it's a lot of work to dial the number, wait for them to answer, leave a voicemail, and hope they call back. Oftentimes, I'm not that worried about them calling back. I just want to get the information to them in a new format in order to get their attention.

> *"Hi _____. This is David with _____. I hope you're having a great week, and I wanted to let you know_____ [information about your "something]. Take a moment and _____ [call to action]. Feel free to give me a call back at _____ or shoot me an email at _____. Thanks so much. Bye."*

Warm connection, information, call to action, and a point of connection. That's it. I make calls and leave voicemails to inform and encourage action...and it works.

Press Release

Because you're starting "something", you'll definitely want to send out a press release to appropriate media contacts. Simply Google "how to write a press release", and you'll find your way. Feel free to quote yourself or write a quote from someone involved, and then have them read the press release to revise or approve their statement. Writing it for them (and getting their approval) is way quicker than waiting around for them to write a few sentences on their own.

Here are four options when you're ready to send it out...

1. **Press Release Distributor (paid)**

    There are numerous companies who will distribute your press release to thousands of contacts and post it on multiple websites. If you have a few hundred dollars to spend, this is a great option. There's a possibility that a news source may pick up your story, but it also gives you good incoming links to your website which will boost your ranking on Google search results. The three companies that I have utilized include PRWeb.com, PRNewswire.com, and ChristianNewsWire.com.

Market Your Something

2. Press Release Distributor (free)
There are also free websites that will post your press release, but it takes some work and can be a bit spammy. Google "free press release distribution" and fall down the rabbit hole of unending links. Another option is to hire someone on Fiverr.com for five dollars to enter your press release in all of these distribution websites. I've done that before, and it is a low-cost way to spread the word.

3. Personal Emails to Individual Contacts
Not only do I use paid and free distribution services, but I also email individual contacts at media outlets that are pertinent to the "something" I'm starting. All you have to do is go to the website of the magazine, newspaper, radio, or TV station, and look for the staff or contacts page. With enough searching around, you'll be able to track down the appropriate person. Email them directly with the press release so that you know you got it into their hands.

4. Creative Object Delivery
Over the years, I've found opportunities to deliver a press release with a creative object that always catches the attention of the recipient. First of all, this works best if you have the appropriate contact name and physical address. Otherwise, you're just sending a package into the office, and it may get lost in the shuffle of all the other mail.

When I was launching a church with a sermon series on building healthy relationships, I included the paper press release inside an inexpensive toolbox filled with tools purchased at a discount tool supply store, and a blueprint poster for the series was attached as well. I hand-delivered each toolbox to 10 local newspapers in our area, and you better believe it got noticed...and we got press.

I've done with same thing with custom-designed cookies, custom miniature skateboards, and all sorts of other swag. Writers and editors at most major news outlets are not allowed to receive something of value that may sway their opinion on a subject, but I've found that low-cost, creative objects are the perfect way to get someone's attention (and possible coverage).

Marketing Calendar
After thinking about a number of ways you can spread the word about your "something", now is the time to put together a calendar in order to give

yourself deadlines. For the sake of example, let's just say that you have an event coming up on March 1st...

January
7th - Website completed.
7th - Facebook and Twitter graphics completed.
14th - Website and social media launched.
15th - Email update mailed.

February
Daily - Social media posts.
1st - Facebook Event launched.
1st, 14th, 21st, 28th - Email update mailed.

March
1st - Date of event.

Although I would anticipate a much larger and robust marketing approach, this gives you a simple example of how you can lay out your calendar - either in a list format (which I prefer) or on a physical calendar itself. Although you may make a draft of this yourself, you'll definitely want to include multiple perspectives and voices to ensure you're not forgetting something.

Be sure to include those who will be implementing the marketing plan in this discussion. They'll be the ones who will be able to tell you what's realistic to pull off within your timeframe.

We Can All Do a Little Something
As a part-time photographer and stay-at-home mom of three young children living in Maryland, Chelsea Hudson was becoming more aware of modern slavery and extremely compelled to take action, but she was feeling less and less equipped or qualified to respond.

Chelsea explains, "I wasn't a lawyer who could donate time to help in the fight. I wasn't a social worker who could hop on a plane and help run an aftercare program. I could barely make it through the day with three kids five years old and under. I felt stuck and useless. There seemed to be this huge black hole between writing another check and hopping on the plane to work in the red light district in Calcutta. I also knew that there had to be a place for someone like me in this battle."

Market Your Something

She ended up searching night after night on the Internet, trying to find manageable and doable ways that passionate stay-at-home moms and working women could engage in the issues. It became clear to her that a curated online resource was needed.

In 2012, Chelsea launched Do A Little Good (www.doalittlegood.com), a website that serves as an online ideas warehouse with education about the issues and a lot of ideas on how to realistically respond in more tangible ways than writing a check to a worthy organization.

The name stems from a quote by Edmund Burke as he states, "No one makes a greater mistake than he who does nothing because he can do only a little." Rather than shrugging off the problem and moving on with the next dirty diaper crisis or carpool pickup, Chelsea resolved to bridge the gap between awareness and action by sharing truly manageable and doable action steps towards greater involvement in the issues of our day.

No matter what tools you utilize to market your "something", remember that they are simply tools. The essence of your marketing is found in your mission, your uniqueness, and your story. Without those three things, you're just spreading random bits of information. In everything you do, you want people to say "yes" to what you're putting out into the world. The key is to share your mission and heart in such a way that people are ready to say "yes" before you even make the ask.

Chapter Nine
REFINE, REPLICATE, REJUVENATE

Even if you only plan to start a one-time project, event, or campaign, you may be surprised to find that leadership and starting more "somethings" is in your future. In order to learn from your experience and prepare for future ones, there are three things I would suggest.

Refine What You've Started
Although you've been "learning" throughout your start-up process, the level of insight you'll have after your launch will be significantly more. Consider asking yourself, your leadership team, and others the following questions...

1. What did the team do well?
2. What could have gone better?
3. What would wish we would have known before starting?
4. If someone was going to do something similar, what advice would we give them?
5. As you look at your own personal performance, what are you proud of? What would you like to change next time?
6. Are there any immediate action steps we should take?

START SOMETHING TO END TRAFFICKING

If you're asking these questions in the context of a team meeting, be sure to have someone capture the answers. Then, when you start your next project, event, or campaign, look back at what you said in preparation. You'll save yourself from making the same mistake once again. If your leaders have teams of their own, encourage them to walk through the same process. It will be eye-opening for the leader and a learning experience for the team.

From time to time, there will be people on your team who don't see eye to eye on what you deem as necessary refinements. Most likely it will have something to do with their own personal investment, and that's okay. Give them grace. Give them time to process the insights of others, and be sure to remind everyone involved of two or three positive things that came out of the situation.

Granted, this process can be a little heavy at points. Your team will feel the weight of what didn't go so well, and there may even be some remorse. Avoid blaming altogether, and instead remind everyone that we're always growing and learning as leaders. It's okay to make mistakes, but the expectation is that we learn from them and refine our processes and efforts for the future.

Two years ago, Elizabeth Alston and her friend, Levi, wanted to help women caught in sexual exploitation in their own city of Portland. Knowing that 82nd Avenue is a well-known "track" where women are sold for sex, they decided to just hang out in the middle of the night to see how they could assist. They soon learned that food and water was withheld by pimps as a means of control and that many of the women didn't even have IDs.

Elizabeth shares, "We quickly gained the attention of law enforcement and have some very funny stories about some of the mistakes we made, but we found a way to approach the women to offer water, hand warmers, something to eat, and a card that has our phone number on it if they want help. The police working on 82nd now carry our cards as well to hand out to women that they pick up."

Last year, another organization purchased a house near 82nd and has given Elizabeth and her team permission to use it for 2 years. They have been working on the house and plan to use it as a drop in center for the women to come in and get assistance with resumes, applying for services, and a safe place to stop in.

Refine, Replicate, Rejuvenate

"We started with what we had - two young adults who care deeply and don't mind staying up all night in a sketchy neighborhood. We live and breathe to unleash a tidal wave of hope in an area that deserves wonder and dignity. We have overcome some incredible challenges, both personally and as a team to see this outreach come to fruition. We continue to be amazed at how people rally around us and serve in incredible ways to make this work. It truly is a team effort."

Replicate Your Leadership
You are only one person, and your leadership is limited. The only way that you have the ability to grow, extend, or duplicate your project, event, campaign, or organization is if you replicate yourself by raising up more leaders. When your "something" has concluded, you have the opportunity to look at your key team members or leaders and ask, "Who do I want to invest in at a greater level?"

Some tangible ways in which you can raise up another leader include...

- Spending more time with them.
- Asking them for input or feedback on key upcoming decisions.
- Reading a leadership book together and discussing it.
- Explaining to them how and why you do what you do.
- Bringing them along to a meeting with your mentor.
- Taking them with you to a seminar, workshop, or conference.
- Giving them more responsibility.
- Discussing the dynamics of team meetings afterward.

It's said that leadership is *more caught than taught*. The question is...how are you going to position yourself and your up and coming leaders to catch what you have to offer?

By the way, you may be worrying deep down inside about your own "position" in the process of raising up others to high profile leadership roles. Remember our conversation about scarcity versus abundance. That applies to this as well. There are an abundance of leadership and serving opportunities and protecting your territory is only going to repel others from wanting to work with you.

If we're going to end human trafficking in our lifetime, we're going to need everyone's support. This heinous epidemic requires leaders to step up and replicate ourselves. It requires all of us to take action, because there is more than enough to be done.

The concept of replication is no more true than in the life of Yvonne Williams. After spending nine months writing a screenplay called "A Dance for Bethany", she and her husband produced a feature film about a 12 year old runaway rescued out of a life of sex slavery and into her dream of becoming a dancer. They sold everything they owned and travelled across the southern US hosting screenings and awareness events.

Recognizing the need for more collaboration, Yvonne coordinated the first Trafficking In America Conference in 2010 and founded Trafficking in America Task Force (www.traffickinginamericataskforce.org), a non-profit organization to motivate and inspire people to use their own talents to create grass roots movements in their areas in relation to ending the tragedy of human trafficking in America. They are in the process of planning their fifth conference and anticipating over 400 in attendance. With offices in four states, Yvonne and her team continue to expand their efforts into prevention education in grades 1st through 12th, an ongoing youth campaign, and an alliance of anti-trafficking organizations.

Rejuvenate Yourself and Your Team
There is a high cost to tackling the issue of human trafficking. For that matter, there's a high cost to leading and volunteering for the sake of *any* cause. For years, I was a workaholic - investing 60-70 hours a week on doing good things in our world. Frankly, my "whys" were kind of mixed up, and I was doing a lot of good things to make myself feel better about *me*. That season of life ended almost seven years ago when I burned out. I couldn't keep running at that pace any more, and I was forced to re-orient my life.

How will you intentionally rejuvenate your mind, body, and soul along the way so you don't face burnout? How will your encourage your team to do the same?

I have found that my health is the most important variable in my ability to be a good husband, father, and entrepreneur. If I'm overwhelmed, anxious, or burned out, I'm no good to anyone. I'm irritable, agitated, impatient, and unkind, and it's not a pretty sight.

In order to cultivate health in my life, I've chosen to...

Refine, Replicate, Rejuvenate

- Check in on my soul health every few days.
- Spend weekly (if not daily) time near the beach.
- Invest meaningful time with my wife and kids.
- Have intensely honest conversations with two or three friends.
- Exercise a couple of times a week.
- Listen to inspiring and spiritual podcasts several times a week.
- Get 8-9 hours of sleep every night.
- Go to therapy when I sense a dramatic situation in my life.
- Decline to work on projects or with clients that significantly drain me.

Your list will look different than mine, but the point is that you need one. How will you intentionally rejuvenate your mind, body, and soul on a regular basis?

There are seasons when I charge hard toward a goal, and I get tired and a little crispy. My wife and I discuss it, and I take time to recharge as much as possible on a daily basis. Then, when the project has concluded, I intentionally refrain from jumping back into another hard-charging project right away. I am learning to pace myself. What about you?

That's something every entrepreneurial abolitionist has to learn - including Lauren Carpenter and Emily Landham, co-founders of t-615, a social enterprise (www.t-615.com) using the art of fashion to raise awareness and funds for the abolition of human trafficking. Started in 2012, t-615 specializes in ethically-made cotton tops and jewelry, and all their supply chains are traceable and offer fair wages.

Emily talks about the challenge and the reward, "The work is hard. The hours are long. The struggles are many. And, all of it is beautiful! Our tribe of artisans, visionaries, farmers, designers, and patrons are all devoted to a common dream, a single tribute: To give respect and affection to our world through ethically-made, beautiful adornments."

Emily is right as she shares how hard it can be. There's nothing easy about starting "something" or ending trafficking, but the reward is worth it.

"Seeing people get excited about the meaning and the beauty of our hand-crafted products brings us a joy we cannot put to words. Employing artisans and paying them what they deserve for their excellent and difficult work is a truly satisfying delight. You pour so much into a dream, you give so much to a desire, to then see your audience rise to the call is a thrill beyond measure."

Emily and Lauren have been re-energized and motivated by the words of William Wilberforce as he states, "We are too young to realize that certain things are impossible... so we will do them anyway."

You already know the tremendous challenge to end human trafficking - whether it be labor, sex, or organ, and *you* are needed. Our world needs you to start "something" to end trafficking, and you have been uniquely gifted to do so.

From your upbringing to one-of-a-kind personality to the good and not-so-good experiences you've had in life, you have been prepared for this very moment. You have access to all the resources you need to accomplish what you're being called to do. There are people who want to join with you, and there are organizations who long to have a leader like you involved with their efforts.

No, you don't know everything, and you're not perfect. You are uniquely you, and you have a heart to help and learn. I love that about you, and I'm cheering you on.

I believe we're in a unique season when young people and old people and singles and marrieds and religious and non-religious are locking arms to say "enough is enough".

Will you lock arms with me and put an end to trafficking in our world? Let's do it together.

ABOUT IN PLAIN SIGHT

IN PLAIN SIGHT is a three-part campaign to help stop sex trafficking in the United States. We are focused on educating the American public on a dark problem that is exploding across the nation and motivating people to take action in their own communities.

IN PLAIN SIGHT: Stories of Hope and Freedom
Executive produced and narrated by Natalie Grant, the documentary features six modern-day abolitionists as they fight sex trafficking across America. Journeying to six US cities, the film opens viewer's eyes to what's happening down the street "in plain sight".

IN PLAIN SIGHT: Devotional and Group Study Guide
After watching the film, individuals and faith-based small groups, Bible studies, and Sunday School classes can use the book to understand and embrace God's heart for the vulnerable and broken in our world.

IN PLAIN SIGHT: Songs of Hope and Freedom
To help fund the work of Hope for Justice, an accompanying music album is available for purchase and features hymns recorded by well-known artists who turn our attention to the hope and healing needed to overcome this darkness. Not only is this an album that can be enjoyed on your own, we hope you'll utilize the songs in a time of weekly worship as you gather with your small group (lyrics included in the back of the devotional/study guide).

Website – www.inplainsightfilm.com
Facebook – www.facebook.com/inplainsightfilm
Twitter – www.twitter.com/inplainsightnow

JOIN THE MOVEMENT

1. HOST A SCREENING
For more information on how to host a screening of the IN PLAIN SIGHT documentary in your area, go to **www.inplainsightfilm.com/screening**.

2. SUPPORT AFTERCARE HOMES
To make a donation directly to one of the organizations featured in the documentary, go to **www.inplainsightfilm.com/donate**.

3. SUPPORT THE FILM
To make a tax-deductible donation to Awaken Media and help us spread the film across the world, go to **www.storiesoffreedom.com**.

CONTACT THE AUTHOR
David Trotter
david@inplainsightfilm.com

Made in the USA
Monee, IL
03 July 2025

20463640R00080